Letters to Eli
My Story, The Story of Many

Delane Cooper
Foreword by Deborah Sinclair, MSW, PhD(c), RSW

Cover artwork created by Susan J. Bird
Book design by Elizabeth A. Kerr, The W.I.T. Corporation

Copyright © 2018 Delane Cooper
All rights reserved.
ISBN-13: 978-1727643336
ISBN-10: 172764333X

DEDICATION

Giving voice to all
the people of experience
who could not find the words

In honour of
Kristen
Mom & Dad
John

Acknowledging those
who give love and support
to people of experience
and may not understand
their friend or loved one

TABLE OF CONTENTS

Foreword	9
Introduction: Letter Writing	11
Chapter 1: Morning Meditation	12
Chapter 2: All Aboard	17
Chapter 3: Manifest Destiny	25
Chapter 4: Choice	33
Chapter 5: Do The Work	42
Keep Writing	51
Chapter 6: The Climb	52
Chapter 7: Give Love	63
Chapter 8: Grandma	71
Chapter 9: The Phone Call	79
Chapter 10: Not My Angel	86
Chapter 11: Pollution	91
Chapter 12: A Knight's Hug	97
The Twine	102
Epilogue	104

I AM
The fire that burns
in each of you
For my flame feeds yours
I AM the wind that
whispers creative seedlings in your ear to
take root in your mind I AM
The land you walk on, the very land
you stand upon at the mountain top
to declare who you are
I AM the water that cleanses your soul
that caresses your skin and freshens the air

I AM
Friend, sister-soul-healer and artist
For I've crawled in darkness
under the blankets of abuse to see
you in the light
For I've cried the tears
for the waterfall to flow to cleanse your soul
For I've curled my body into a ball
writhing in pain to fit into the palm of a butterfly
so you too can fly
For I've soared the skies waiting
for each of you to join me

I AM
Friend, sister-soul-healer and artist
For Metal allows me to create
sacred wearable space
For Stones allow me to connect
you with the earth and its energy
For Words allow me to communicate
the story that is within you
For Art allows me to offer my hand to you
to dance with me

J AM
Friend, sister-soul-healer and artist I AM

-Delane Cooper

ACKNOWLEDGEMENTS

I am grateful to have had this experience of sharing my story through this book and to the many people who were patient, took a deep breathe and politely asked if I needed a time out while I wrote this book. Grateful to The Universe for bringing the right people together at the right time so I may learn, grow and be.

To John for experiencing this journey with me; it truly has been and is love in action. To Kristen for your love. To Mom and Dad for encouraging me to be more even during times of tough love. To all the Veggie Ladies in particular, Dee, Eleanor, Sylvia and Valerie who were stand in mums and mentors. To Pearlaso who allowed me to shed tears without judgement.

To Mary Aitken for creating a club called Verity. Without Verity, I would not have ever met these incredible women who have lifted me up. To Laurelea for encouraging me to tell my story. To Deborah and Sara who have guided me in sharing my story. To Lynne for hugs of encouragement. To Elizabeth, Jennifer, Michelle, Rula, Sam and Sandra for being incredible cheerleaders. To Rona for being generous with her time and support. To Jody for having the patience to listen. To Joan for inspiring me to tell my story by sharing hers with me. To Gail for teaching me the importance of sharing one's soul. To Caroline for checking up on me. To Rosie for her bright smile. To Del, Bonnie, Mary, Barbara, Mary, Barbara, Susan, Catherine and Elaine for the support and laughter. To the many other sisters who have picked me up and dusted me off when I have fallen.

To Mary and Bruce Vachon for opening their hearts and being supportive friends.

To Bill Fulghum for listening with an open heart and helps me see joy in the world through art and nature. To Stephanie Gairdner for believing in me and gently guiding me through difficult times. To Valerie Campbell for helping me to consider other points of view in how I perceive the world. To Shauna Bean for your love and support. To Genya Nee, Winnie Shi, Lina Witzel, Sarah Hawco, and Minelle D'Souza for reminding me to dance. To Claire Garber for being my penguin spirit sister and together we will help save animals around the world. To Rachel Tucker for calling it as you see it. To Marie Wong for your optimism.

To Kelsey Matheson-McCord, Melissa-Jane Shaw and Shannon Barnett for being inspiring and beautiful souls. To Tina B, Delia P, Robin C, John B, Salvador F, Patrick F, Tara M, Homaya A, Rita S, LaShaun C, Tamara R , Elisabeth S and Mirna B for your generosity, kindness and humour.

For being in the company of Tara Sutton and Genevieve de la Reux who inspire me to push myself beyond my perceived boundaries and to give voice to a trauma that is happening to children around the world.

To all the participants of the art project who generously shared their raw stories with me and inspire me to do the work I am doing. To all the supporters of My Story, The Story of Many.

To Cynthia Richards, Jackie Eldridge and Elizabeth Kerr for being generous with their time, skills and guidance in encouraging me to reignite the art project, My Story, The Story of Many. Words cannot express how especially grateful I am to Jackie and Elizabeth for their generosity of time, commitment in helping me see this book realized and walking with me through this journey so the project becomes an art exhibition. To Susan Bird for creating the artwork for the book cover and expressing the layers of my life through collage with much love and care.

To all the people of experience from childhood sexual abuse and childhood trauma. Know you are not alone. Know you are stronger than you're trauma. Know that asking for help is an act of courage.

I am grateful to all the individuals that were not named for personal reasons. Some were family members, some friends, some mentors and I wouldn't be surprised if others were angels.

In gratitude with love,

Delane

FOREWORD

Thanks to all the excellent research recently focused on the neurobiology of traumatic stress, we now know that trauma lives in the body. No matter how much of our story we consciously remember, our body remembers it all. Our body provides a roadmap to our struggles. If we befriend our body, reclaim our body, treat our body symptoms as allies, and listen to our body talking to us, then each of us can heal our core wounds.

Delane helps us do that. She shows us the path.

In *Letters to Eli: My Story, The Story of Many*, Delane courageously takes that journey inside. Delane shares her journey with grace, raw grit, and bravery, but also with care and compassion for her readers.

Beautifully written with an exquisite tenderness for her beloved Eli, Delane's book gifts us with insight into what it is like to be betrayed as a child, dismissed as a teenager, and revictimized by those in positions of power who should have known better. Finally, she reveals her path to finding an ally who does what other professionals should have done—name her abuse as a crime, take the right steps to hold her abuser accountable, and help her to find safety. Ultimately Delane finds herself embraced by a loving family who embodies the traits of the kind of family every child in this world deserves: security, safety, trust, unconditional love, respect, ongoing connection, and a willingness to be there for us even through the toughest of times.

Trauma literature tells us that silence, shame, lies, and disconnection are the tools of the predators among us. Healing transcends trauma through the opposite measures: by telling the truth thus exposing the lies, creating connections, allowing love in, breaking the silence, speaking out, and drawing strength from the knowledge that we are not alone.

As a therapist, I have listened to countless heart wrenching disclosures of intimate details of the atrocities people endure at the hands of predators. These encounters open up sacred spaces. Sharing the tears, the shame, the rage, the disbelief, and the grief within a trusting, connected relationship is the first step to healing core wounds. And then I watch very closely and the miracles begin to happen.

The beauty of being a witness as someone gathers their strength, finds their authentic voice, and embraces their courage to withstand the tough process of healing is indescribable. I am honoured to witness the joy of transformation.

I am often asked if I find my work depressing. I answer with a resounding "no." When I accompany a victim of abuse—journeying with them through the release of the pain to the other side of witnessing their transformation from victim, to survivor, to thriver, and lastly, to warrior—I know I am walking alongside our future leaders. Breaking down the walls of shame, realizing we are not alone, watching people finally "get" that the abuse was not their fault, is liberation in action. Witnessing people become who they were always meant to be is a beauty to behold.

Delane's book is a gift to us all. Writing her life story has been a healing journey for Delane. Sharing her journey with us is an antidote to silence and shame and disconnection. Delane permits us to accompany her into the depths of her despair as a beautiful innocent child who is tortured relentlessly, and into her reclaimed strength and power as she escapes and discovers allies, a loving family, friends who believe in her, and a circle of supporters who uplift her.

So dear reader, get your cup of tea, take a deep breath, quiet your mind, and settle in for a story about the power of transforming tragedy into strength, beauty, and joy.

Thank you Delane for giving us a story of hope. The world needs your voice!

Deborah Sinclair, MSW, PhD(c), RSW

INTRODUCTION: LETTER WRITING

There are times when writing a letter eases one's mind, especially when sharing uncomfortable truths of the past. In my case, writing to my child was easier than communicating in person. Writing a letter allows me to get my thoughts out without having to worry about dialogue. As I get older, some dialogue is not only uncomfortable; it requires stoic authenticity. These days I worry if I am being authentic enough or am I being too authentic. Authenticity requires vulnerability. I'm cool with being vulnerable when I share a story but I have come to notice that it is the listener who becomes uncomfortable. It is obvious through their body language and/or facial reactions. It's the reason I prefer writing letters – I don't have to bear witness to the other person's discomfort when receiving my story whether challenging, joyful or loving.

It's difficult to read a person's body language these days. With the advent of the Internet, coaching classes, mentors and all of the therapy available, I'm afraid of misinterpreting body language as more and more people are coached on how to outwardly communicate. In a face-to-face dialogue, curiosity and worry consume me as I find myself wondering if the person I'm with was coached. Is the individual responding a certain way by the tone of their voice when presented with new information? Are they a psychologist? Did they take a mindful meditation course to listen with healthy boundaries and/or is their response authentic?

These letters to my child, Eli, are the conversations I wish I could have had in person but chose to write instead.

✳✳✳

Many of the names have been changed in this book.
Eli – pronounced as in the boy's name Eli with a long i (eee-lye).
Filipino references include:
Nanay (nuh-nye) – mother
Tatay (tuh-tye) – father
Lumpia (loom-pia) – spring roll

Clarity comes from action, not thought.
– Marie Forleo

CHAPTER 1: MORNING MEDITATION

Dear Eli,

Today is Monday. I hope this letter finds you well. I realize that I could have connected with you by e-mail or text but seeing that I have not spoken to you in decades, I thought a hand-written letter would be best so there would be no pressure to reply. It's kind of ironic that I used the Internet to locate you but not to communicate with you. It is an interesting observation, but I'm sure you would agree. Unless, I hear from you otherwise, I hope you're fine with me sharing my thoughts with you now that I've moved to the country. The country offers so much time for reflection. The robins and blue jays don't judge me if I put the recycling out this week and the sunflower grows on the dirt pile despite not being planted by me.

Being a Monday, it seemed like a good time to start using my time productively on the train ride into Toronto. This time on the train provides me the opportunity to start opening the door to the hidden museum of experiences that reside within me. Eli, grab a tea or coffee and sit outside at a park or on your porch, if you have one. I ask that you be open to the journeys I share while I escort you through my soul's museum.

A couple of years ago, I decided to meditate by the pool at a club where I belong. After two years of not taking time to meditate because of the stress of my job and a boss who required mandatory and auxiliary time of my life, meditation seemed like the right place to begin. To begin – again. It's difficult not to berate myself for beginning all over again as I approach the half a century mark. If someone had told me that creating new beginnings happens often and not to attach a number to it, maybe I wouldn't have been so anxious about the number of beginnings that I've created to get me where I'm sitting now. By the pool, there is a rattan-framed sofa with comfortable supporting cushions. This is where I usually sit and meditate. Do you meditate, Eli? Do you know what meditation is?

The last several months were difficult on my husband and me, since I had fallen into a depression after leaving my job two weeks before Christmas. This fresh start did not make up for time lost with family and friends, time not working out in the gym and robbed of time experiencing joy in life. Needless to say, life was upsetting and devastating. I found it difficult to move on and let go of my anger. I was stuck. Now, it was time to meditate. It was time to accept responsibility for the victim role I had played all of these years.

When I left my condo, I headed down the back stairs and through the hallway on the main floor. I walked with purpose knowing that my new meditation practice was going to be the beginning of something. I didn't know what, but I knew it was something. People like me have to believe in something, someone or some entity outside of ourselves. It helps people like me to continue on. It's what got me through my childhood to be the person I am today. I acknowledged our condo concierge with a smile as I quickly walked by. He was engaged with another tenant musing about the happenings over the past weekend. When I turned to walk up Jarvis St, a chill ran down my spine scolding me for not dressing warmly enough. Toronto in March is traditionally cold where a toque and scarf are required. However, in the last couple of years there have been, what I call bonus sun days. The sun is out and tricks my mind that it is warm enough to not have to bundle up. Today was not one of those days. Though the sun made its grand entrance in the morning, it was quickly whisked away by dismal grey clouds.

Passing the office building on the northwest corner, I peered to the left to see if the elderly lady was sleeping in the park under the trees near the sidewalk or if the regulars were seeking the protection of the park's gazebo. I enjoy routines when they are mine and I have created them. People, even the ones I do not know personally, are part of my visual scape. They take on unknowing acting roles in the movie that is my life's routine. The elderly lady must have gone for a walk since her bags were still in sight. The park's gazebo had its guests, as there was a patchwork of colour on the podium validating that people were present. Further up the street, a corner of the park was peppered with reminders that dog owners were not being responsible. I don't know if you have a dog, Eli, but I loathe irresponsible dog owners, especially when it comes to public shared spaces.

Though the streetlight was red indicating to stop, I crossed the street anyway since there were no cars coming down the one-way street. As I passed the sushi restaurant, I reminded myself to note the dark space between the restaurant and hotel to see if anyone was there. The light between the two buildings had been out for several days and a couple of men had been using that spot as a meeting place. Though I could not hear what they were saying, walking by them made me uncomfortable. Fortunately, this morning no one was there. As I crossed another one-way street, I passed an empty parking lot that butts up against a dilapidated building. It seemed not that long ago, when it was white and clean, and I was speaking to a lovely young Ethiopian man about renting a car. He explained that the landlord no longer wanted the car rental business there, so it became vacant and run down. Today, the building is tattooed with graffiti and garbage accessorizes the property. A tall wire fence stands along the perimeter of the property just shy of the public sidewalk. Not only do people change; places change and sometimes not always for the better.

Instead of walking all the way to the corner, I cut through the muffler repair shop's parking lot proving to be a poor decision on my part because there was ice everywhere. As I shuffled my feet across the ice to the sidewalk, I hurriedly continued on as the cold wind was biting my face. After a few more steps to the club, I pushed the heavy door open, entered the vestibule and walked past the concierge desk into the coat closet. As I hung my coat, I noticed that only a handful of members were at the club by the number of empty hangers in the closet. When I emerged from the closet, the concierge and I exchanged morning greetings and I made my way down the stairs to the locker room.

When I entered my niche of lockers, I was delighted to see that locker 99, my favourite locker, was not taken. I placed my bag in the locker and retrieved a robe and slippers. After I changed out of my street clothes and slipped on the robe, I headed to the pool area. There is something special about walking into a warm room with a pool in the morning to meditate. The ozonated pool provides a place to gently focus the eyes prior to closing them for a formal meditation. I seated myself on the cushion, planted my feet on the stone tile, straightened my back and placed the back of my palms on my knees. I focused on a space just above the pool, took a deep breath in, let it out and then closed my eyes. Traditionally, meditation is a technique to quiet the mind. However, on this particular morning, meditation would be the prelude to watching the movie behind the curtain of my eyes. This movie had been archived in my soul's museum for decades.

✳✳✳

It was early in the morning on a school day before breakfast and I was in the room behind the kitchen at the ironing board ironing my white collared shirt and my pleated tartan skirt of red, green and white. The room was a former bathroom with a working toilet and a large army green washing machine next to it. In front of the washing machine was the ironing board and above it the wooden medicine cabinet missing its mirror. The light was a single light bulb on the same wall above the medicine cabinet with a pull string to switch it off and on. Even on the tips of my toes, I could barely reach the string but after several attempts I would stretch or jump to turn the light switch on, so I could iron. The space between the ironing board and the washing machine was wide enough for someone to stand and iron. I don't recall ever having a step stool or I would have used it. The room never smelled clean to me not like the rest of the house. I don't know if it was the fact that the toilet was hardly ever used and the water sitting in the bowl for months on end contributed to the strange scent or if there was mould in the room. I hated ironing because of the smell. I was too young to know that I could have dragged the ironing board out to a more open, fresh-air space. Even Nanay didn't iron in there. She would fold a twin-size bed flat sheet into a large rectangle and lay it on the floor in the main hallway to iron. I didn't do that because my grandma taught me how to iron shirts on the ironing board. The front and back panels of any buttoned-down shirt only look good when properly pressed. It's the narrow part of the ironing board that helps get into the shoulder area of a shirt, so it can be ironed to a flat clean finish. The crisp pleats of my uniform skirt were only that way if ironed on an ironing board, pressing one pleat at a time, so the plaid pattern matched horizontally when the skirt was held up. If grandma ever came to visit and saw that I was lazy in my ironing I would be scolded with words and a tone of voice that would make me feel smaller than I already was. I dreaded ironing my skirt. When finished, I unplugged the iron, turned out the light and went into my room to finish getting dressed. My green cardigan was on the bed to complete my Catholic school uniform. The year was 1979. Margaret Thatcher was elected as the first female Prime Minister in the UK and I was in Grade 4. Once the uniform was on, breakfast finished, backpack packed, it was off to school.

On this particular day, each student received a book and a form, which was to be signed by a parent to acknowledge that we were going to learn about human reproduction. The form was signed marking the beginning of my abuse.

✳✳✳

When the mind is quiet for meditation, it is fascinating to see what is revealed. Why tell you now after decades have passed between us, Eli? I don't know why. Maybe it's the number of self-help books that I've read over the years suggesting that I learn to live without regret. Maybe it's the social media posts of a serene image adorned with a quote about having no regrets in life. Maybe it's how a secret moves within the body. Over time, the secret no longer resides within the membrane of a cell; it escapes the cell, then bounces from one muscle to another and later gains momentum to take residence in an organ. It starts to poison every cell with its darkness. Maybe, it's time to reach out to my child and share my truth.

My train is pulling into Toronto, so I will leave you with what I've written today. I don't expect to hear from you immediately but hopefully, you will find it in your heart to reply. Seeing this is my first letter to you, I will not presume to say, 'with love'. It seems appropriate to say, 'until we connect again'. So, unless you disagree, it is what I will do.

Until we connect again,

Delane

With the new day comes new strength and new thoughts.
– Eleanor Roosevelt

CHAPTER 2: ALL ABOARD

Dear Eli,

My train into Toronto was a little late this morning due to freight train traffic. Now that I'm settled into my seat and have my herbal tea, it felt appropriate to pen another letter to you.

Thinking it was going to be easy to write, I find myself distracted by the person behind me. He is on the phone deciding to have a leisurely catch up call with a buddy for the rest of train passengers to hear how awesome his life is. I immediately take out my headset that is plugged into my phone so that Mozart can drown out the awesomeness going on behind me. When I look up I notice more passengers with their earbuds or headsets on since the train left the station. As I scan the immediate view, I notice tired eyes, take in the sad eyes, gloss over the vacant eyes and smile when there is life in a passenger's eyes. What's even more refreshing is when someone smiles back. This morning no one smiles back.

There is a young woman across the aisle one row in front of me who is staring out the window with sunglasses on as she drinks her morning coffee. The way she sits reminds me of me when I took my first train ride at the age of 17. At the time my arms were folded in front of my torso suggesting to anyone curious that I was closed off to the world but inside I was yearning to be part of the world. It is interesting to observe someone else's sitting position and how it can trigger a memory. Now I have something to write.

I thought I would need to write a couple of more letters before I started sharing the depths of my soul, but I'm practicing communicating sooner than later so there is no time like the present. It is my hope that, by authentically sharing my experience of what happened to me as a child, you'll find it in your heart to be open to welcoming me back into your life, possibly as a friend. If not a friend, then at least we can mutually accept and respect each other's existence.

Though it may seem mundane, it feels appropriate to share with you what I remember of my early years at Catholic school with each grade leading up to the fourth grade which had its own highlights.

✸✸✸

In first grade, we were learning about guppies and other life forms that lived in a small 4-litre tank. The tank did not look like a happy place to the eyes of this first grader. It had green plants floating on the top, stones on the bottom, the darkness of water and the unknown beings moving in the water. One tank for each of six children was placed in the centre for the group to observe. Prior to the group being assigned a tank, Sister Clare instructed students to rearrange our desks to form a cluster in lieu of a large table. The group's guppy tank was placed in the middle of our cluster half on my desk and the other half on Ronald Rivard's desk.

When we were asked to draw what we saw in the tank, Ronald lifted the hinged desk top to retrieve a pencil inside resulting in the tank's contents being emptied. There was a combination of water, long slimy greenery and live, moving beings squirming around on my jumper! While the others thought this was the funniest thing, and Ronald was wondering why our classmates were laughing, I felt like people were laughing at me because of my wet jumper and socks. Sister Clare did her best to find paper towels to dry my clothes off but if you've ever worn a tartan jumper, you'll know that the material can get quite heavy when wet. Hoping to make me feel better, Sister Clare pulled out the Friday surprise box of treasures. It was a shoebox filled with various riches to remind us that life was precious, and we owed gratitude to God. Being presented this box was a big deal, because each week one person was selected based on good behavior or above average performance in marks to pick something out of the box. I was asked to pick a gift out of the surprise box on this particular day; it was a Wednesday, not a Friday. It was not for good behavior or performance, but as a vehicle to stop me crying, since I was wet and not sure if the living beings were dying stuck to my jumper.

Sister held the treasure box above my head, so I could not see inside. I placed my hand on what felt like a good treasure. I was instructed to share what I had fished out of the magic shoebox. The thin white cardboard box held a solid object. When I pulled it out of its box, there was a gold plastic frame of a headshot of Jesus. Jesus, our Christ, was looking off to the left with a halo of light around his head. Sister Clare wrapped her tiny arm around me and asked if I liked it. With a nod of my head indicating yes, I went back to my seat. For the rest of the school day I felt like a soggy day-old tuna sandwich in a plastic bag. If anything good happened in grade one, it was overshadowed by this incident.

When I was in grade two, I learned how to crouch under the desk during an air drill and how to stand in a doorway during an earthquake. These skills became important life-saving tactics for us as seven-year-olds. In religion class, I learned that I came third. God came first, my neighbor second and I came third. My neighbor according to my teacher were actually my parents, family members, even my brother, friends and others. 'Others' to this second grader meant everyone else in the world that was not part of the former. Little did I know that putting myself third would be so ingrained in me that it became a strong thread of my internal fabric. This golden thread affected my decision-making well into my adult years. Grade two was the year to learn how to fear the environment where I lived and those people I could or could not trust.

In grade three, music class was the most engaging activity for the class as a whole. I remember a fellow student named Michelle, who decided to incorporate hand gestures into the song, "His Banner Over Me is Love". The music teacher loved it so much that the rest of the class had to mimic along. The boys of the class never looked forward to this song as they were embarrassed to raise their hands over their heads in the shape of a rainbow as they sang "His banner over me" and then place their hands over their heart to the words "is love." It reminded me of the love I had for the musical group, The Village People. I loved them because of their costumes and I looked forward to this song in music class. I pretended the boys were auditioning for The Village People. It was in grade three where I used my imagination at school for fun and at home to pretend to travel to other worlds especially through books.

Grade four was filled with many new beginnings. Beginning number one was our teacher, Ms. Rakel. She was, not only our academic teacher, but she was our music teacher too. Not only did she sing but she played the guitar! I was star struck by her awesomeness. Unlike my other teachers, Ms. Rakel taught me that she could do more than one thing – she was a teacher, a singer, guitarist and a dancer. She was multi-talented. Music class was more fun than third grade as we learned songs like Tingalayo, Puff the Magic Dragon, If I had a Hammer, My Grandfather's Clock and of course, my favourite despite having no clue at the time what the words meant, Blowing in the Wind by Bob Dylan. New beginning number two was the first time that we learned how to dance as a class. Square dancing became a class the girls enjoyed and the boys merely tolerated. What was interesting about square dancing was that we had to pay attention since each move was dictated by the caller. One had to know how to move when called, "Bow to your partner, bow to your corner," "Weave the ring," or "Do si do."

After months of learning the various moves, we were invited to dance with Ms. Rakel's square dance group outside of school. At least she told us we were invited but upon reflection, she probably asked her square dance group if she could bring her grade four students who were keen on showing off their new skills. It was fun to dance with the adults. They seemed delighted to have us as their guests that night.

New beginning number three was the introduction to the Boxcar Children books. Fantasies of living in an abandoned railroad boxcar in the woods filled my head. How I wished for similar adventures to whisk me away from the everyday life I found myself living. The newness of being introduced to so much creativity was exciting. It was the first time I enjoyed waking up and going to school.

One day, on our way home from school, my brother Aron asked if he could stay at our cousin's house for the night. I replied that I didn't care but that he had to call Tatay and ask. I didn't mind Aron going to our cousin's on a school night as I liked having the house to myself. What I did mind was that I had to get Aron's uniform ready for the next day, so he could go to school directly from our cousin's. When we got home, Aron made the call and Tatay approved his weeknight sleepover. Next on my task list was to get Aron's pajamas and school uniform packed. For that fresh, crisp, clean look, our uniforms were always pressed the morning of but seeing Aron was off to a sleepover, I had to gather his uniform in preparation to iron. For no wrinkles on our green cardigan sweater, a damp cotton cloth similar to a flour sack cloth was placed on top of each section before applying the iron. Sleeves first, front panels next and back panels last. Once flattened, the sweater would be flipped right side up to button the front of the sweater, then flipped again with buttons facing the ironing board. Folding the arms back made the crease one inch from each shoulder. The next fold was the bottom of the sweater up one third, then once again, so the sweater was folded into perfect thirds. I would then turn the sweater over to ensure the perimeter was a perfect square with the V-neckline symmetrically in the centre. The white collared shirt was ironed in similar fashion to the sweater with the exception that close attention had to be paid to the corners of the triangular collar. Folding the bleached, crisp white shirt followed suit – square and symmetrical. Lastly, I had to press the grey pants. Ironing pants is straight forward providing that one could feel the side seams then match them to iron a crisp clean fold down the centre.

It occurred to me, while ironing, that my mother would not be coming home that night. She was in the hospital again for another surgery to remove a cyst. I had to get a form signed and return it the next day. Thinking nothing of it, I left the form in my backpack and didn't bother taking it out. Aron's clothes were packed, along with his homework, and off to our cousin's house he went.

I was left to make dinner on my own and complete my homework. I made one of the few dishes I could easily cook without supervision – pork chops in Campbell's mushroom soup also known to me as poor man's stew. It was easy to make – cut the meat off the bone into little cubes, chop onions, slice mushrooms and throw into a frying pan with a bit of vegetable oil. Cook until the pork had a crusty brown coating. Open a can of Campbell's mushroom soup, pour into frying pan, add 1 cup of water, stir, then simmer for 20 minutes. Serve over steamed white rice for a tasty and filling meal. Steamed rice was a cinch to make since we had rice cooker. I was taught to fill it up to the second line from the bottom and add the water to the pot using my middle finger as a measuring stick. I had to dip my finger into the rice to see if it came up to first fold in my knuckle. If it did, I would place the tip of my finger on top of the rice and fill the pot with water to the same measurement of the fold of my knuckle. After I had finished eating dinner alone, I washed my dish and flatware, placed the leftovers into a Pyrex dish and washed the frying pan. Rice in the rice cooker was left on 'warm' so when Tatay came home all he had to do was heat up the stew.

I learned to be friends with solitude and silence. It took practice over the years but as with any relationship I knew I would have to invest time in befriending solitude. There were times I wish I had a cousin close in age to pal around with like my brother did. He was lucky enough to have sleepovers at my cousin's house during the school week. I did not have anyone with whom I could share those times.

After I finished my homework, I turned the television on to watch a rerun of Green Acres but my favourite character, Wilbur the pig, wasn't on the episode so I turned it off and picked up one of my Nancy Drew books. After reading a chapter, I had heard the lock to the front door turn indicating Tatay returned home from work. He came up the stairs and asked if dinner had been made. I replied, "Yes." Then remembered the form that had to be signed and mentioned it to him. He nonchalantly told me show it to him after he ate. I returned to reading my young sleuth's adventure for a couple of chapters. When I had noticed that Tatay had turned on the television, I brought him the piece of paper to sign. He reviewed the form and asked if I knew what the form was about. I nodded yes as my answer. He then requested to see the book that was referenced in the form to be signed. I handed him the book. As he flipped through it, he asked if I knew what any of the illustrations meant. My reply was, "Not yet." Feeling nervous and noticeably uncomfortable for the first time around Tatay, I said that our teacher explained that our parents had to acknowledge we were going to start a sexual education class. He signed the form.

The evening routine was next – washing my face followed by brushing my teeth. After I spit out the toothpaste and rinsed my mouth with cool tap water, I headed to bed. I climbed into bed, pulled the blankets over my chest, freed my arms from beneath the covers, made the sign of the cross and said my evening prayers – one Hail Mary, one Our Father and repeated the phrase, "I am third. God is first, my neighbour is second and I am third".

Sometime in the middle of the night I remembered feeling the rumble of the train a block and a half away making its regular nightly visit on the steel rails of the island's belt line yard. Trains had always intrigued me because *they took people places, carried big things, at least in my childlike mind they did and, most of all, I had never ridden the steel horse. For as long as I could remember, the nightly Del Monte train schedule was part of my sleeping routine.*

The next morning, while I was getting ready for breakfast, I recalled having a dream and being asked to get on board the iron horse. It was a great dream! The conductor seemed kind and gentle. He offered his hand for me to climb on board and I eagerly accepted his invitation. The train car was empty and the conductor indicated that I could pick any seat I wanted. When I took my seat, I had a feeling the ride was going to be magical. Peering out the window, we were travelling across a beautiful, blue ocean where large fish were jumping up from the water and flying through the sky with a smile on their faces. One of the large fishes looked right at me and I returned its smile. The wheels turning on the steel rails caused a gentle rhythmic bounce of my chair. My dreams became better than any experience I could ever imagine during the day. Flying fish that smiled were definitely magical.

✳✳✳

Did you have magical dreams as a child, Eli? Do you dream now and do you remember them? If so, I would love for you to share what you dream. I dream and I do remember them.

Looking back, that dream was my first experience disconnecting from my physical body. Dreams became a way for me to escape what was happening to me after the midnight hour. It's interesting how coping mechanisms develop at such a young age similar to a train's timetable. Eli, please indulge me here for a moment with this odd analogy.

The train takes the same route that has a point of origin and ends at a destination at the same time, just like a habit that has the person doing the same thing over and over again to get the same outcome. When the train is early, the result can lead to a happy passenger at the location of arrival. However, a late train can turn a commuter into a disgruntled passenger due to heavy freight train traffic, malfunctioning electronics, track maintenance, or a fatality on the tracks. On the flip side, a late train could be an opportunity to make a new friend who is sitting next to you, get more work done or write letters like I am writing to you, Eli.

Based on the severity of the travel advisory, arrivals can be delayed anywhere from five minutes to four hours. Similar to the many challenges affecting a train's timetable, triggers on my journey of life can lead to a pleasant, surprising outcome like a key learning about myself or it can be an outcome that feels real in its devastation, like the shame that weighs on the body. As you can see, situations like seeing the young woman sitting across the aisle mentioned earlier in this letter can prompt memories of the past.

As my mindset and body have become healthier and stronger over time, I have learned to turn the bad habits I practiced when triggered into something productive. I used to retreat into myself and or mindlessly daydream as coping mechanisms. However, with practice, meditation and intentional dreaming became my source for strength and creativity.

It's time to go as we're close to Toronto.

In gratitude for listening,

Delane

I can be changed by what happens to me. But I refuse to be reduced by it.
— Maya Angelou

CHAPTER 3: MANIFEST DESTINY

Dear Eli,

After a long day at my studio, I'm back on the train to head home. I find it easy to write to you while on the train. Writing to you is a great distraction from work and it helps me focus on something else versus getting annoyed with the child three rows in front of me, yelling at the top of his lungs. I, along with the other passengers I am sure, are all hoping for this weary child to take a nap. Ironically, however, what may be closer to the truth is that many of the adults on this train likely need a nap even more than that child. As a passenger, it's hard to appreciate the exuberance of this child because he's so full of life and merely testing out his lungs.

Prior to boarding I was waiting in line at the train station and noticed a young girl with her family. Marketers would identify her as a tween, that age between a little girl but not yet a teenager. Tweens in North America are interested in the same things as a teenager such as fashion, music and friends but, unlike the typical teenager, tweens still want to spend time with their families. This tween had long, straight black onyx hair tucked neatly behind her ears to highlight her youthful face. A thin-strapped purse draped across her body like the ribbon that a beauty pageant contestant proudly flaunts. She was wearing a fitted white t-shirt with a unicorn on it that covered her upper body and slim-fitting denim jeans to cover her legs, and stylish sandals that I wish I was wearing instead of my gold-coloured sneakers. I smiled with approval as if I was a judge on some random fashion channel. When our eyes met, I held my smile and she returned the smile but then

I had to look away. Her eyes triggered me to a time when I was in grade school.

It's curious that a look from a child today could so easily create a flashback to my own long-forgotten childhood memory.

✳✳✳

Let me take you back to grade school again. My interest in history class was non-existent although I knew it was a subject where I'd be measured on how well I could memorize dates, events and locations. In grade seven, my sudden interest changed when Sister Mary Thomas taught us about Manifest Destiny – the doctrine or belief that the expansion of the United States throughout the American continents was both justified and inevitable. According to Sister Mary Thomas, Manifest Destiny was the driving force in the industrial age. It was Manifest Destiny that drove tycoons to build a railroad to connect one coast to the other at all costs. The railroad had to be built without any care for human rights nor environmental impact on the land. Sitting in class, the words Manifest and Destiny sent a chill up my spine, because I resigned myself that it was justified and inevitable that my body was no longer my body, just as the land that belonged to the Indigenous people no longer belonged to them – nor to Mother Earth.

The person who took my body was not the tycoon that Sister Mary Thomas spoke about. Instead it was Tatay. As we read about the tracks being laid across the land to connect the Atlantic coast to the Pacific coast, I felt every railroad spike being driven into my body as the invisible tracks of abuse were being laid on my body, not only trapping it but also trapping my mind and soul. The rest of the day was cold and I remember staring at my notebook and tracing the words Manifest Destiny over and over, then re-writing them on the pages that followed.

After history class, it was time to prepare for Sunday mass by going to confession, which happened on Fridays. There were set times for each grade to attend. Along with the rest of the good servants of this earth, we sat in the pews thinking about what we were going to confess to the priests who were chosen in their rotation. Confession was a weekly routine which didn't require much serious self-reflection in grade seven. The offenses to which I would sheepishly admit were fighting with my sibling, talking back to one of my parents or not wanting to do homework.

On this particular Friday, it was Father O'Malley's rotation and I knew what I wanted to say.

When it was my turn, I walked into the open room for a face-to-face confession. The side entrance behind the right aisle of the Basilica served as the room for this in-person meeting for those who boldly dared to look a priest in the face to confess their sins. Father O'Malley greeted me with a warm smile and asked me to sit in the chair that was angled in such a way that I was not sitting directly across from him but slightly off to the side where we could speak to each other as if we were in someone's family room in front of a fire. I shyly smiled and took my seat.

Father O'Malley was tall when he gave his sermons in front of the congregation and he still seemed tall in his important chair as a representative of God. The entrance was white with large walnut colour doors. So much light was coming through the windows that warmth and safety seemed to fill the air. As I took my seat, I immediately went into the ritual of "Bless me Father for I have sinned…" then I paused. Father could sense my angst and said, "Continue my child." I took a deep breath and said, "Bless me Father for I have not sinned but my Tatay has."

At that moment, there was a sense of relief that I told someone who would help me figure out what to do next beyond saying my three prayers of Hail Mary and three prayers of The Lord's Prayer for help and guidance. What followed were two simple questions: "What are you saying, child? and Who is Tatay?"

"Tatay is my father. My Tatay touches me in the way that we were taught in grade four was wrong but I was too scared to tell anyone."

"I see," he replied and let out a heavy sigh.

We both sat in silence. It felt like I could have read a chapter of a book during that extended period of silence. With both hands, I rubbed the hem of my tartan skirt in between my index finger and thumb in an attempt to fray the stitching of the hem as I desperately wanted something to do during the silence. Tears welled up and one by one they escaped my eyes. Like good little soldiers they marched one behind the other to form a line of protection. After several rows of soldiers had been released, Father shuffled in his seat as if to ask for order or in a silent way conveying 'pull it together child.' I straightened up in my chair and awaited my instructions for penance. Slowly and softly Father O'Malley spoke, "Sometimes our parents know not what they do. Have you told anyone else? Have you told your mother?" My voice was silenced by my thoughts as I nodded my head to indicate that no one else knew. A cloak of shame delicately came down from the heavens landing on my shoulders.

Suddenly, I had the realization that I had sinned by being selfish and going against the Fifth Commandment to 'Honour thy Mother and Father.' It was in that moment that I feared I had done something terribly wrong by telling Father O'Malley. I cast my eyes down for disgracing my family in the eyes of God and a representative of God. "Tell your father to come and see me. In the meantime, if it happens again tell him it's wrong and that he should stop. Ok?" "Yes, Father" was all I could say. He forced a smile then instructed me to say one Hail Mary and ask for God's help and guidance.

As I got up from my chair, I felt like iron chains had been added to my cloak of shame making it difficult to walk out of the room. My hope of being saved vanished. I put my hand on the large, brass door handle and thought of turning around to make one more plea to Father O'Malley but, instead, pushed the door open and left the entrance of hope.

As I approached the altar to say my prayers, I could feel my black, green, red and white tartan, pleated skirt sway as if to the rhythm of a drum, the kind of drumbeat that soldiers march to when carrying a coffin for a military funeral. I knelt down, with hands clasped together, placed my wrists on the church rail and I looked up at Jesus on the cross behind the large imposing altar. I pushed my bony knuckles into my forehead as if to silently punch myself in the head. After the silent, self-beating, I looked up at the altar, which beckoned me to come up and offer myself up as a sacrifice. Instead I bowed my head and said my Hail Mary. A tear, like a dutiful little soldier, escaped the trenches of my eye then another followed as I asked God for guidance.

✳✳✳

I share this particular experience with you, Eli, because it taught me to not ask a real human being for help; ask God. Help became an internal endeavor. Allow me to continue my story of grade seven, one that occurred months after my confession to Father O'Malley and you'll see what I mean.

✳✳✳

Another school day was missed – maybe due to a cold or the flu; I could not remember what I was told, but I was sick again. My absent days from school were opportunities for me to dream and dream I did. The train would come and the nice conductor would invite me on the magical ride. Invisible railroad tracks only made sense in my dream state because the iron horse would smoothly glide across the ocean. Never before had I seen a dolphin jump over the train and wink at me before entering the water. I remember orca whales racing this iron horse called the train. Fish flying at window height beckoned me to wave and, at times, open the train car's window to speak to them to pass the time of day. These fish were quite the little story tellers. The train never crashed or sank. I would always wake up back in my bed. When I woke up, Tatay told me that he was going to work and that Nanay would take my temperature again when she came home from work.

I slept while waiting for Nanay to come home. It was only another couple of hours to wait alone in bed. Alone. Alone to dream. I did dream but this one was not like the train dreams. Instead, I found myself in an all-white room with a bed bisecting the room at the corner as if to draw a 45-degree angle in a square. No windows were to be found just white walls. When I looked at the bed, the body I saw looked familiar. I floated closer to the body and thought how strange that I am in the bed and floating at the same time. As I retreated from my body in the bed, I noticed there were tubes hooked up to both arms but did not know why. Then red started going through the tubes and my blood was spilling on the white floor. Frightened that my body didn't know what was going on, I screamed to myself, "Wake-up! Wake-up!", but the body in the bed was not waking. The pools of blood were getting larger on the white floor and a fear set in that my body would never wake up. I floated closer, whispering this time, "Wake-up. Please wake-up". When I woke up, I was in my uncle's arms who was carrying me down the stairs. I could hear Nanay's voice pleading in a panic to the next door neighbour, "Please watch Aron. She has a high temperature and we need to go to emergency."

My uncle commanded Nanay, "Hurry. Get in the car! She's burning up in my arms!"

The slamming of the car doors were a far distant muffled sound that I heard despite the fact that I was actually in the car. When I woke up, I was on a gurney in the emergency at the hospital. There a doctor gently asking, "Can you hear me?" He had his palm on my forehead bringing some comfort to my confusion about where I was when I opened my eyes. The room was a soft and white, unlike the stark, cold white in my dream. Despite my lips being dry and my mouth feeling like a farm field that was in desperate need of rain, I quietly replied, "Yes".

Two or three other team members accompanied the doctor, so the room was filled with a buzz fueled by a sense of urgency to make something happen. I could hear the pitches of other people's voices, but I couldn't see everyone. The doctor told me that he was going to gently lift my head and see if I could touch my chin towards my chest. Immediately after he rocked my head forward, the pressure in my neck was unbearable and I let out a cry of pain. A nurse was drawing blood out of my left arm; I could feel the cool steel of the needle piercing my skin. I don't recall the other poking and prodding they did to my 12 year-old body, but the last thing I do remember was the spinal tap. I was directed to curl up into a ball. As the male nurse was explaining what they were about to do, he placed both of my hands in his and closed his around mine like an oyster safely keeping a beautiful pearl inside of its shell. The cold swab could be felt in circular motion in a particular area along my spine. The nurse said 'Now we need you to be brave. We need to get some fluid out of your spine to find out what's wrong with you. "Whatever you do, do not move out of that curled position until I tell you it's ok." My eyes communicated that I understood; many fearful soldiers were waiting in case the call came to be released from the eye duct trenches. The nurse nodded, and the doctor made a lumbar spine puncture with a needle that felt like a fiery red, hot samurai sword fresh from the fire pit. The screeching shrill I made caused the nurse to hold my hands tighter as she commanded me not to move. But the shock of having something foreign in my body sent panic signals throughout my body like the emergency siren going off for an earthquake. I must have jerked my body because all I heard was, "We have to do it again, the tip of the needle broke." Without a command, the fearful soldiers were stampeding down my face and dropping onto the gurney to protect me from more pain, but it was fruitless. The second puncture sent me into myself, as I prayed for my beautiful train dreams of flying fish. I went deep into the chasm of fear. Now silence was my only response. The soldiers continued to march, but no longer stampede down my face.

The doctors took what they needed from me just like Tatay took what he needed. I did cry. I closed my eyes to call on my train dreams but all that appeared was darkness behind the lids of my eyes. In this dark space, I asked why – hoping the God I prayed to at church would come down a golden escalator from heaven and answer me. Instead, a fog of shame engulfed me like a fog in the early morning lingers over a marsh and the surrounding farm fields. In this fog, the realization that socked me in the stomach was that this is my punishment for speaking to Father O'Malley about Tatay. I opened my eyes to see Tatay with his hands on the rail of the gurney and his head hanging down. With eyes closed, the words Manifest Destiny came to mind and I lulled myself back into the chasm within me to find rest and hopefully sleep.

✳✳✳

I was diagnosed with bacterial meningitis. I was away from school for more than a month. When I look back, Eli, I believe that I internalized what was happening to me and made myself sick. How could I do that, you might ask seeing that I was only a child? I didn't know it at the time, but I was abandoning me and my self-worth and allowing something like a virus to check-in and take over my body. In some ways, I think I internalized what was going on in the hopes that someone would be curious enough to inquire about what was really going on. No adult expressed curiosity. A blessing did happen though. Tatay didn't touch me for that entire month. There were no train dreams with dolphins or flying fish during that time, but that was ok. I dreamt of other things like becoming a cheerleader in grade eight.

You know what's interesting, Eli? I kept all the Get Well cards from my seventh-grade classmates. Ever since that confession with Father O'Malley, I wanted to matter to someone and these cards were proof, in my childlike heart, that I mattered. If I didn't matter to the rest of the world as an adult, then there was a slice in time when I mattered enough for all of the students to make me Get Well cards. It is partly these cards that have helped me to stay resilient all of these years because they reminded me that I did matter even when I felt I didn't matter to the people who were supposed to love me.

Today, the feelings of emptiness and not mattering no longer linger because I know I contribute society and make a difference to the lives I touch. Belonging to community has helped which is the reason I continue to volunteer, find new interests, develop and maintain friendships, invest time in my marriage and most of all maintain a healthy diet, exercise and meditation. Do you think you matter? One day, I'll hear from you, Eli, and when I do I hope it's facing each other over a cup of tea. It is important for you to know that I'm writing these letters to you in the hopes that we may reconnect.

As with any good story or conversation, this one must come to an end as we are approaching the station.

In gratitude for being open to listening,

Delane

We don't develop courage by being happy every day. We develop it by surviving difficult times and challenging adversity.
– Barbara De Angelis

CHAPTER 4: CHOICE

Dear Eli,

It's such a beautiful Friday afternoon that I made the easy decision to take the early train home! Julia Cameron, author of the Artist's Way suggests taking artist dates. Though I cannot go on artist dates to the gallery or museum, my artist date is leaving the studio early to take a leisurely jaunt through Berczy Park on my way to the train station. It's an extra 10 minutes to myself and it's enough for me to deem it an artist date. Today, I found a bit of shade under a tree to get a bit of a reprieve from the hot, intense sun we've been experiencing of late. Closing my eyes, the sound of a river's rapids come to mind but when I re-opened them, I realized that it was the fountain's water spraying from these larger-than- life dogs spitting up towards the grand prize – a dog bone. Layering on top of the spraying water with such velocity was the sound of children laughing as they climbed on top of or pet these canine caricatures and have their pictures taken by happy, jovial parents enjoying the afternoon.

Off to the left of the fountain towards Front Street was a mother and teenage daughter arm in arm waiting to have their photo taken by the younger brother, while the father appeared to be admiring the fountain and its sculptures. Too bad the photo will not turn out as they hoped. A dark shadow was cast on the mother and daughter's faces seeing the afternoon sun was behind them. Realizing the dark shadow on their faces was enough of a trigger to cut my artist date with myself short and continue on to the train station.

Shadows seem to lurk in unassuming places like in the middle of a bright, sunny day that can bring the shadow within me out. I call this shadow Ego. Over the years, Ego has taken on a male persona because of my experiences with men who have passed judgment on me. From telling me that I'm not pretty enough, or I'm too short, or not smart enough, or too smart or sometimes I'm just not his type because I'm not the right colour and his family wouldn't approve.

As I made my way to the train station, Ego was sitting on my left shoulder wagging its finger at me saying with a bit of a taunting tone 'Tsk. Tsk. Too bad you didn't have a loving Nanay." Ignoring Ego's comment, I, along with the many other adults being herded by time and the green streetlight that indicated it was safe to cross, entered the intersection with a sense of urgency in our step so to not miss our bus, train or subway.

When I noticed my gate started pre-boarding, I fished for my phone in the open sea that was slung over my shoulder called a handbag. Bag yes; hand-sized, definitely not, as I chuckled to myself. Physically multi-tasking by walking towards the gate, adjusting my handbag on my shoulder, with my right hand holding my phone, pushing the button that turned my phone on and then swiping left with my thumb to get to the app for my train ticket. I double tapped the screen to enlarge the image so the ticket agent at the gate could scan the QR code. Grateful that the ticket agent was a familiar face, he smiled, scanned my ticket and waved me through. Up the escalator I went and noticed my left shoulder feeling heavier than the right. Though the Ego is not physically visible and tangible in weight, Ego's weight is real and at times he may as well be Mike Tyson, the heavyweight boxer.

The train platform is loud with rumbling train engines so the agent at the top of the escalator confirmed my train number and motioned with his index and middle finger the direction of the train. I follow as directed and cannot wait to take my backpack off. The weight of a laptop, linen scarf, phone & laptop charger, toothbrush and toothpaste are heavier than it should be despite removing the 3 design books and 2 reference books on meditation. As I approach my train, I recognize one of the service attendants and she smiles. With the wave of her arm, she welcomes me to her car. Up the stairs I go, find my seat and relieve my shoulders of my handbag and backpack. Prior to sitting, I unzip my pack, remove my laptop placing it on the seat next to me, zip the pack shut and place it in the overhead compartment.

Pleased that I'm on board a bit early, I got myself situated in my little 50cm x 72cm world so I can now write to you, Eli. The train departs the station after the herds of passengers have boarded and I am over the moon that I do not have to share my two-seat row with some unknown traveller. With relief, I place my right hand on my left shoulder and try to massage it as I tilt my head to the right for a bit of a neck stretch.

Now that the service assistant has served me my tea, I now can address Ego's comment about Nanay. He's still nearby but no longer sitting on my shoulder. His idea of fun is to send me telepathic needling messages of how I was not loved enough by my biological mother.

Unbeknownst to the young photographer the shadow cast on his mother's and sister's faces while having their picture taken at the park near the water fountain earlier is similar to the shadow that was cast upon Nanay and me. The young teenage boy wanted to capture the CN Tower, the water fountain and, of course, his mother and sister – all the elements that should make a great photo telling the story of a beautiful Toronto afternoon. Things are not always as they appear. For instance, the not knowing about lighting that can tell a different story in a photograph just as it's in the not knowing of an outcome that could change a story.

Let me share with you how Nanay's decision affected my life as I know it. But first, Eli, I must take you back to Grade 10, when I was 15 years old.

✻✻✻

After years of abuse at the hands of Tatay, I decided I had enough, so I ran away. Where I went does not matter, however I did return to my hometown and showed up at my friend's house. The two of us were in her bedroom talking about what I would do next. The law of the universe already knew what it had in store for me; I was the actor who would fulfill the role of the universe's written play. The house phone rung, my friend picked it up and acknowledged the other person on the phone call. With a hesitation in her voice, she acquiesced and the word OK could be overheard. The receiver was returned to the phone's cradle. She turned to me and said, "'Your father is coming to pick you up. What do you want to do?" I shrugged my shoulders, resigned to the fact that I had no other plan. The anxiety was building up in me and I could feel the heat rise from my back, up my neck, making my head unusually hot and causing me to perspire at my hairline.

What should have taken at least 15 minutes seemed like only 15 seconds since the phone call. The doorbell rang and my friend allowed me to open the door to see Tatay. He seemed taller that day because of the anger that was raging within him because I had run away. He ordered me to the car and as I walked through the threshold, I turned back to meet my friend's eyes with a plea, 'pray for me'.

My god didn't help me before, so why would I ask help from a god with a prayer from my friend? The only answer that resonates true today is habit. It was a learned habit from a young age to pray for help.

Once in the car, many loud words pierced my ears coming from the driver's seat in our short car ride home. The gear-lever was shifted into park and with the turn of the key, the engine no longer rumbled nor hummed. I looked out the window and saw the house I lived in; the same house I no longer wanted to be in. Tatay exclaimed, 'Get out! Now go see what you did to your Nanay by running away.'

My hand pulled the car door handle towards me to release me out of the four-wheeled prison. First my right foot on the curb followed by my left foot. With my left hand, I carefully launched myself off the passenger seat and out of the car. I contemplated slamming the car door out of sheer frustration due to the situation I found myself in, but knew it would do no good other than make a loud sound and my ears were tired of hearing loudness. They longed for quiet and solitude. With respect to the car, I closed the door being careful not to slam it, since it was not the car I was angry with; I was angry with myself. Me. Just me.

Tatay directed me to walk towards the house first and up the porch stairs as he walked behind me, probably to ensure I wouldn't turn around and bolt to escape the invisible talons one's family can dig into one's back without knowing the talons even existed. He unlocked the front door and I marched up the steps to our second-floor Victorian apartment. As I marched up each step, I heard the front door lock behind me noticing there were no salty soldiers in stand-by mode to run down my face. When I reached the landing, the stairs turn left and I motioned my body to follow the flow of the stairs. While still on the landing, I could hear the capiz shell wind chime above my head, rattling. This startled me because of superstition which said if placed near the entrance of a home, a capiz shell wind chime would catch any ghosts entering into the home and be trapped in the chime, forever trying to get out, but never finding a way. I believed the ghost that was to save me (or be a supporting angel) was now forever stuck in the wind chime. The feeling of real aloneness came when I took the first step from the landing.

As I approached the hallway of our apartment, Nanay was curled up on the living room sofa which faced the steps perfectly in full view for me to see her swollen face marred by makeup that had not been removed and hair unbrushed for two days. She was wearing her housecoat over clothes. Maybe she was cold, but it was warm outside, so the layers of clothing confused me as the windows to the apartment were open. When my feet touched our hallway floor indicating I was formally in our apartment, Tatay firmly said, "Let's all sit in the family room and talk there."

I ruefully looked at the framed photograph of the tower designed by John Galen Howard. The runaway letter was no longer held within the frame. How ironic it was that behind me was a capiz shell wind chime and in front of me a tower that housed a carillon of a twelve-bell chime. Tatay had told me years ago that inscribed on one of those bells was: We ring, we chime, we toll, Lend ye the silent part, Some answer in the heart, Some echo in the soul. As I cautiously marched towards the family room, I knew for whom the bells tolled. No silence was lent in this moment; the answer was in my heart; the echo shames me to my bitter soulful death.

The corner of the sofa was my choice of seat. There was a wall behind me in case the universe thought that this would provide a great slapstick moment for an oversized hammer to bonk me on the head to wake me up from this diabolical, cartoon hell I was cast in. To the left of me was the large four-foot, wide-open window which invited the much needed breeze through its six-inch opening as more sweat beaded at my hairline. Nanay sat on the opposite side of the sofa with her feet on the sofa and knees up to her chest like a child who was ready to rock herself for comfort. Tatay sat on the corner of the rectangular dark oak wood veneered coffee table. He was bent over with head down and his elbows on his knees holding the upper part of his body up.

He lifted his head, stared at me with angry eyes and challenged me in his calm, ridiculing tone, "See what you have done to your Nanay? Explain yourself."

I looked at Nanay and wondered why she is the one curled up as a child who needed to be comforted when it should have been me? The years of hot confusion was under serious pressure inside of me when I directed my question to her.

"Did you even read the letter I wrote to you?"

Her eyes filled with red anger as if I insulted her intelligence suggesting she didn't know how to read English. She retorted back. "Of course, I read it! It didn't make any sense."

Two hyenas who happen to be my parents were cornering this sun sign Leo, me. The lion in me was crouched down waiting with impeccable patience and I held my silence before answering her.

Impatient, Tatay slammed his hand on the coffee table and ordered me to answer Nanay.

From the hunched shoulder position receding into the sofa cushions, my body came to attention at the virtual vibrations that rippled within these four walls. This lion was not retreating into a cave; I was out of the cave and I was ready.

Turning to Nanay I roared back at her. "If you read my letter, did you ask Tatay? Did you ask him what he's done? If you did not, ask him now!'

She glared back like I was a lunatic, but she faced Tatay with a sense of urgent understanding cried out, "What is she talking about?"

This lion didn't wait for its prey to ask for forgiveness and once again I roared at her, "Have you ever wondered where he was in the middle of the night? Did it not ever occur to you why it was ok for you to go out and gamble your weekends away? Because he was in my bed! Yes, your husband, my father in my bed!"

Bewilderment now consumed Nanay's body for my accusing words had to have shocked her. There was no reflective moment to be had by Tatay. Just as a hyena has no time to think if its own life is worth is saving, it moves by instinct to get out of the way of the lion.

With face turned away from Nanay as if offering his cheek to be slapped by his wife, he quietly said with no remorse, no tear, no anger, "Yes, what she's said is true."

Nanay reached across the cushions and engulfed me in her arms with her tears baptising me. Instead of being cleansed of original sin, I was being cleansed of fatherly sin. Tatay left the room.

After Nanay and I shed all the tears that could be shed, the two of us found ourselves sitting on the sofa staring out the window in silence no longer holding each other. Truth has a way of separating people based on how they interpret the truth.

She turned to me and asked with sincerity, "Why didn't you tell me?"

In a monotone voice the words that flowed from me were 'You were too busy gambling, too busy working, too busy doting over Aron and you were too busy being sick.' The latter may as well had been a dagger I stabbed into Nanay's heart. The number of cysts that had to be removed, in and out of hospital visits for this surgery or that surgery even post hysterectomy. I dressed her bandages while having to look at some draining tube coming out of her abdomen after one surgery. While she was sick in bed, in grade school I ironed my brother's and my uniforms, I cooked dinners and I was Tatay's entertainment or stress release. I was tired of being tired. Her eyes held back the tears as her eyes appeared glassy when I looked at her.

Flatly she asked, 'What do you want to do?'

Without hesitation I uttered with an exhausted, raspy voice from all the crying 'I can't stay here anymore. I need to sleep somewhere else.'

'Ok. Pack your pyjamas, clothes for school and toothbrush.' No emotion. No hug.

Moving robot like, I got up from the sofa, left the family room where we all acknowledged we were no longer a family. I went into my bedroom to pack up the school books for studying and reached for the small duffle bag under the bed to pack a small lot of my personal belongings. When I was finished, I sat at the top of the stairs of our hallway waiting.

Nanay came out of her bedroom properly dressed. She indicated for me to stay there and wait so she could brush her hair and wash her face. Minutes later, I heard the washroom door open, so I leaned back to see her emerge from the room where she normally comes out with a smile and painted face. This time there was no smile, no make-up. She looked white as a ghost with eyes so swollen no amount of cold water would help bring the swelling down. The purse that was hanging on the newel post of the staircase was removed and she placed the strap over her shoulder then quietly murmured 'Let's go.'

Before she went down the stairs, a shadow came over her face. She paused, looked at me with a forced smile, then led the way down the stairs.

✳✳✳

Eli, this shadow was similar to the shadow cast on the same mother and daughter I saw earlier today at the fountain. Sometimes a situation or something I see provokes an uncomfortable emotion in me and many times it's difficult in the moment to understand why I am feeling the way I am. Hence, why writing these letters to you is helpful for me to explore and safely re-visit the past events.

✳✳✳

When Nanay and I left the house that day, a fleeting dream came to me like a staccato note in Mozart's Symphony No. 40 in G Minor. The two of us were going to drive somewhere and start a new life together without my brother and without Tatay. The reality was we drove to a family friend's house. Nanay chose to have me stay with her. It's where I stayed until I moved into my foster home.

✳✳✳

Looking back, I don't know what it would be like to be a 37-year-old mother from the Philippines in a western world for only seventeen years with limited family support. I can't imagine what it would be like for her to be faced with choosing between me, the child she gave birth to, or the man she had married who forever changed her daughter's innocence.

I have spent thirty-three years being angry with her for making the wrong choice. As I am writing this to you, Eli, I am just realizing that it was the most courageous thing she ever could have done. Read that last line again slowly and digest it if you can. By not choosing me, she gave me the freedom to grow as I should have and did. I have had thirty-three years to re-think what love from a mother and father means because I've had the opportunity to have foster parents who later took me in as one of their own. Maybe, the price to pay was giving me the only gift she could – freedom. By letting me go, she gave me the opportunity to have thirty-three years to work on healing the memory in my body, the hurt in my soul and the confusion in my mind. Most importantly, I have thirty-three more healthy years to be – me.

This is one of those times where reframing an experience after time has passed can be a healthy perspective to embrace.

I've been suffering from headaches lately due to this heat and my body is overwhelmed with new emotion that leaves me somewhat perplexed from sharing this particular story with you, Eli, especially now that I have taken this opportunity to look at Nanay in a different light. It's this light that will help me turn the tide of darkness in my lion's cave, deep within my heart. It's interesting when I look at the past with a different lens coupled with a little bit of realized hope, love or forgiveness, Ego slips away quietly into his lair.

Will write soon.

In gratitude for listening,

Delane

Every great dream begins with a dreamer. Always remember, you have within you the strength, the patience, and the passion to reach for the stars to change the world.
– Harriet Tubman

CHAPTER 5: DO THE WORK

Dear Eli,

Today is Wednesday and the train has left the station. It seems I have settled into a comfortable, yet familiar routine writing to you on the train. I know it has only been a few letters but being on the train writing to you reminds me of the safe like feeling I felt when I was a child on a train in my dreams. Granted, I am now riding a real, train where no flying fish are smiling at me outside my window, yet the rumbling of the daily train ride bridges the feeling of security I had after the midnight hour.

Do you enjoy reading, Eli? Last Friday a friend gifted me, Victor Frankl's Man's Search for Meaning. It wasn't until this morning on the ride in that I decided to read the first several pages while enjoying a cup of tea. It seems strange to read about another one's life and how the account of theirs seems relatable to mine, even though our lives couldn't be more different. I know nothing of what it's like to be a young doctor with dreams and aspirations. I do, however, know what it's like to be a child with dreams and aspirations. I know nothing of what it's like to serve in a prison with death looming ever so close. But I do know what it's like to be a prisoner in my own body. I know nothing of what it's like to have lived, endured, survived and written about one's observations and accounts while being in a concentration camp. Yet, I have experienced trauma within the boundaries of my own family. Now, I am sharing my personal account and hope it will help others who lived similar experiences.

What I do know is that we both chose something outside of us to keep us going. For me, at age 15, I believed I was destined to be more and bigger than I could ever imagine; it was my imagination that saved me. I imagined a life where I was free to be me. Anyone who has listened to motivational speakers today know that, in order to achieve your dream, there are no shortcuts. You have to do the hard work.

Eli, I am chuckling as I write about this topic because I'm going to share with you my version of doing the work. Granted, it was no laughing matter at the time and it still isn't today, but I have such gratitude for time.

✸✸✸

In grade eight, my teacher was Sister Mary Ellis. Several classmates seemed to have an upper hand in class as Sister Mary Ellis taught their older siblings. In many cases, I think this brought some solace to Sister, since she would be familiar with the status of their families and how they contributed to the parish. As I didn't have that sibling opportunity to pave the way for me, I used my creative talents to work with Sister Mary Ellis. I really wanted her to like me.

When I look back at how we interacted, I think she was unsure how to communicate with me as we sat together over creative projects. I just kept hoping she'd notice something. During the school year, I had the opportunity to decorate our classroom door with a poster I had designed on butcher paper. At Christmas, I created a large Santa Claus popping out of a wrapped box with his Christmas list, complete with all of the student's names in hand. Strangely, I proudly created the artwork, installed the poster on the door and then took a step back realizing I forgot to place my name on Santa's list. Silly me.

I plowed through the school year happy that I was going to graduate. After being a cheerleader, playing both volleyball and basketball, I was happy for school to be over. To get out of the house, I volunteered at local convalescent homes and enjoyed spending time getting to know the residents. Many of them seemed generally happy, at least to this eighth grader.

On one bright sunny Saturday, I agreed to help out in an art class. A very tall woman with dark sunglasses and white hair neatly pulled back into a ponytail entered the art class in a wheelchair. I looked at the coordinator and she smiled and greeted the woman, placing her right at my table. I recall quietly asking the coordinator how would she make art if she couldn't see? Without skipping a beat, she grabbed my hand and introduced me to our participating artist. The artist asked me to tell her which colour paint was in the tray. She asked me to tell her when she made a mistake with her colours and help her. I happily agreed.

Witnessing this artist paint was an incredible experience. When she finished, she asked if I liked it and I exclaimed, "Yes!" I then asked her how she could paint something so beautiful without seeing. Gallantly, she replied behind her dark sunglasses, "To appreciate beauty, one does not need to see to create." Her nurse politely waited for her to finish her response, then smiled and pushed this beautiful woman back to her room.

Every Saturday after that, I was excited to be with the artist who had captured my heart. Then one day, when she was not in attendance, I asked the coordinator where she was. "I'm sorry, honey, but she passed away earlier this week." I felt numb. I walked to the Basilica that Saturday after art class, entered the house of God, found an empty pew far away from the alter and said a rosary on my own for the incredible person I never saw again.

I think experiencing this death touched my heart more than the passing of a relative. Her death had such a profound effect on me. I never forgot that we should always paint regardless of whether we can or cannot see. Paint a painting or paint a life; the artist unknowingly taught me to paint. When I made that realization, I knew I had to make plans to seize my canvas and brush.

Several weeks later, I graduated from grammar school. With graduation came the graduation party at school, followed by a party at home with family. For graduation, I made my own dress with white eyelet for the sleeves and a finished white eyelet ruffle for the hem. The dress was from a McCaul's pattern and I was pleased to have found a bright aqua blue satin sash to complete the look. Without my grandmother's watchful eye, I tried to follow the pattern, but sadly made the sleeves a bit too big so they kept slipping off my shoulders if I hunched over. This forced me to stand straight and tall so the sleeves could sit on my shoulders. Since the pattern was made for the average-sized girl, I neglected to consider that I was several inches shorter than many girls my age. Sister Mary Ellis told Sister Margaret Delaney that I made my graduation dress. Having Sister Mary Ellis' acknowledgement was a gift unto itself.

I sometimes wondered if she had some inkling that family life at home was not easy. Just before our graduation ceremony, Sister Mary Ellis took me aside to tell me I was going to be presented with an award for the volunteer work I had done throughout the year. I was stunned that I was being recognized as I thought no one at school even knew I volunteered at the convalescent homes. I proudly nodded my head then rejoined the class to enter the Basilica for our formal graduation mass.

After the ceremony, my family went back to the house and there was a celebration with relatives. Nanay had made a wonderful feast. When it came to family gatherings, it never mattered how poor we were. Somehow, my parents always put together enough money to entertain in true Filipino style – lots of food on the table. The amount of food always seemed excessive, but it is the Filipino way to have leftovers and send the visiting families home with them. I suppose it was a way to say thank you for coming. The dining table in the kitchen became the community buffet table for the family to enjoy the feast. Extra table sleeves were inserted to lengthen the table. A white tablecloth was put on the laminate dining table and covered with a plastic clear table cloth to protect it from food drippings. At times, it would be a bit tricky arranging the dishes because the plastic cover had burn marks on it. Nanay would stand back to ensure the platters were rearranged to cover the burn marks while still displaying everything in a lovely balanced manner of presentation of colour and texture of food.

Fish stew with bitter melon was usually served in a white bowl or large steel soup pot. Warm tuna spinach salad with diced tomatoes was presented in a lovely glass bowl. The dishes that Nanay made seemed like they could feed a city block. The platter of lumpia would not be the ordinary, simple lumpia of ground beef, raisins and potatoes. Hers were extra-large lumpias, twice the size of standard hot dogs, filled with chicken, shrimp, bean sprouts, cabbage, carrots, green beans, celery, onions and garlic. The chicken had to be minced not ground; the shrimp was whole so that when one bite into it, there was a surprise pop of flavours: carrots minced (although she didn't know that's what it was called here in North America), green beans bias cut, celery cut into pea-size pieces, onions finely chopped, and garlic minced. The chicken and shrimp were cooked and the vegetables were added and cooked to al dente so when the lumpia was deep-fried, the vegetables were never over cooked.

Making lumpia is an art. The cook makes lumpia to entertain the oral senses with flavour and texture. If lumpia is made correctly, it's nothing like a Chinese spring roll. It may have been inspired by the spring roll, but they are not the same. The lumpia maker goes to great lengths to make a golden, crispy roll beautiful outside and inside so when you bite into it a burst of colour and flavours are revealed. A great lumpia tastes great on its own, but for those who have discerning taste buds, sauces are made to accompany them – from spicy hot to salty, vinegary but not sweet. Nanay always welcomed the compliments for the large Debuque ham perfectly quilted with whole cloves and topped with caramelized pineapple rings. However, if a relative complimented her on her lumpia, that was when she was most proud. Nanay was not one to make our nightly dinners during the year, but when she cooked to entertain, it was fabulous. As she took pride in her cooking and presentation skills, she also took pride on the illusion that we were a happy family.

After the last guest left, Nanay deemed the graduation party a success. Relatives came, food was enjoyed and I had received several financial gifts that were to go towards university, which seemed like an out of reach goal at the time.

The summer continued on like the previous four summers. Each day melded into one big Catholic horror story. I regularly questioned myself what I did wrong all these years to deserve such a dysfunctional relationship with my father. Why is it that I can't really remember playing with friends? Could it be that I didn't play with other children because I was told to stay home and I was the toy being played with?

It was a late June summer afternoon and my brother was playing at our cousin's house scheduled to return home at dinner. Knowing there was free time available, Tatay used it as a "play" period with me. He told me I was sick and to stay in bed. Once he satisfied his desires, he left my room as I lay there feeling degraded once again. I had reached my limit and I knew I could not take this treatment anymore.

Immediately, I grabbed the cheques and cash from my graduation and I stuffed them into my orange ski coat. Although it was a hot summer, I knew I needed a warm coat since the outdoors were soon to be my new bedroom. With jacket on, a pair of jeans and a tee-shirt, I headed down the stairs to leave. I got to the lower staircase and there was a very angry Tatay behind me. As I tried to open the door, he slammed it shut and locked it. In a desperate fight for freedom, no amount of kicking, screaming or biting was enough for my captor to let go of this now broken-winged bird. The little hot soldiers ran down my cheeks, but anger and frustration fuelled my determination to continue to fight. However, even my flailing body was not enough for him to drop me. Bound by his arms, I was carried up the stairs to the 2nd floor landing and thrown on the floor. My head hit the spindle that kept a strong line on the wooden stairs. Pain now travelled from my body to my head and I could feel it swelling.

Then I heard my brother's voice through the mail slot of the apartment door. "Can someone open the door?" As I lay on the ground working to muster up the courage to sit up as my head was still ringing from being jarred. I could hear Tatay saying something to Aron. I realized that if Aron was upstairs with me, the torture might stop. I screamed repeatedly for what seemed like several minutes, "Aron, get up here! Come up stairs now!" I heard Aron ask Tatay what was wrong but I could not hear the answer as I was crying in pain and imploring Aron to come inside the house. Then, the front door closed and the lock was engaged. My war cry was not enough. My captor returned to the landing, picked me up and threw me on my bed. I found myself on another mechanical horse journey with only the distraction of the flying fish and jumping dolphins.

As the old saying goes, 'If at first you don't succeed, try, try again.' Try again I did. This time I decided that I would enlist the support of my school counselor on the last day of school in grade nine. I'll save you the precursory stuff because it does seem unbelievable at times, but here is what happened next.

I went in to see the counselor during first period and didn't even report to class. I sat in her chair and asked for her help. This is how our dialogue went.

"So, tell me what you need help with, Delane."

"I need help to leave my family."

"Oh?"

"My Tatay, my father in English, has been sexually abusing me since grade four and I can't take it anymore. Will you help me?"

There was a pause on her part and after a long sigh, she sat up straight and with an upbeat voice said, "I'm sorry that this has happened to you. Well, let's see how the summer goes and we'll deal with it when you return in September."

Dumbfounded for a moment, I was in a state of confusion because I thought school counselors were supposed to help students. I got up from my seat in silence, not bothering to ask for a hall pass to return to class and went straight to the washroom. I entered a stall and vomited.

✳✳✳

As you can imagine, Eli, my trust in adults had been completely rocked off the precipice with no bungee cord to bring me back. At least that is what I thought until grade ten.

✳✳✳

One morning, I decided to go to my first period class early and bring Gord a cup of coffee. Many of the students called him Gord, short for Gordon, rather than addressing him formally as Mr. Jackson unlike the other teachers in the school that were addressed as Mr., Ms. or Mrs. Gord liked getting to school early to prepare for his day, so it was not unusual to find him in his classroom 30-40 minutes prior to class. With two cups of coffee in hand, I turned the handle of the door and, as luck would have it, Gord was sitting at his desk.

"Morning, Gord!"

"Morning, Delane! Thanks for the coffee. I didn't get a chance to stop by the cafeteria to pick one up."

"No problem."

He placed the coffee on the corner of his desk so as not to spill any on the papers he was correcting. I could never understand how he could read any of the homework with his dark sunglasses on, but he did. I sat in my seat, which was five seats back from Gord's desk parallel to the classroom windows that were open to let the fresh morning air into the classroom. I think he did that to make sure all the students would remain awake for class.

"Hey, Gord. Mind if I run something by you?"

"Shoot, kid," as he looked up from his papers taking a sip of his coffee.

"I'm no longer living with my family. I'm staying at a family friend's house."

Gord removed his sunglasses, placed them on the stack of papers and replied with, "Oh?"

"My father has been molesting me since I was in grade four. I finally told my mother that's why I'm staying with a family friend. My question though is should I go to the police?"

In a tone of seriously trying to comprehend the gravity of the situation, Gord said, "So let me get this straight. You're telling me your father has been sexually abusing you since you were in the fourth grade?"

"Yes. So, do I go?" I asked, wondering if I had made the right decision to confide in Gord.

He was my debate and public speaking teacher. He was a teacher I trusted and one who encouraged me to be my best He even walked me through what constructive criticism was so I wouldn't be afraid of it and could hear what was being said because it was meant to improve my speech or position in a debate. If someone would guide me in what the right thing to do, it would be him.

"Actually, as a teacher I am obligated to report this to the police. So, before I do this, you need to be sure what you're telling me is the truth."

My eyes welled up with tears and with relief in my voice I explained that he was the first person since grade seven who has taken what I've said seriously.

"Thank you."

It felt as if a one-hundred-pound weight had been lifted off my shoulders and with that I placed my elbows on the desk and allowed my hands to cradle my face as years of cries for help had finally been heard.

Gord got up from his desk, walked over to me and placed a hand on my shoulder to offer comfort. 'Stay here. I'm going to lock the classroom door, so the other students don't come in and see you crying. Try to pull yourself together while I go make the call. There is a box of tissues in the third drawer of my desk. Go and get it. I'm really sorry that you had to go through this for so long in silence."

✳✳✳

Eli, I had a dream of escaping my family situation. However, a dream is only a fantasy unless you do the work. I did the work of asking for help numerous times. I also did the work to simply survive. I coped by managing to turn in homework, playing sports and cheerleading. I did the work by helping take care of my mother and brother. Now, I no longer wanted to do the work of remaining silent. I did the work to believe in me.

Today, I am filled with many dreams and aspirations. In order to achieve them, I need to continue to do the work and be patient, not only with time, but also with myself for I know by experience that if I do the work my dreams will be realized.

Eli, I realize that these letters may be too 'raw or authentic' but know I share my stories with you because I have waited too long to reach out to you.

In gratitude for listening,

Delane

Dear Eli,

I keep writing because I believe that you are reading them. If not you, then someone is getting some entertainment out of what I've been sharing and the individual does not have the heart to tell me that you do not exist at this address.

Until next time,

Delane

Change and growth is so painful. But it's so necessary for us to evolve.
– Sarah McLachlan

CHAPTER 6: THE CLIMB

Dear Eli,

It's been quite a while since I've written. It's easy to stop writing when one gets stuck in one's head. I have to admit that sometimes I enjoy the monotony of the train ride in the early morning to experience the subtle bounce in my seat vs. watching my computer screen dancing to the hum of the wheels turning on the rails while trying to work.

I am curious to know if you measure your life by career milestones, age or experiences. Maybe one day you'll share with me your thoughts on this subject. As for myself, I would say experiences mark my milestones. The idea of measuring my life by age messed with my head because I was constantly comparing myself to others and their accomplishments by age. Logically speaking, this comparing of oneself is ludicrous. Socially speaking, I was conditioned by my parents, school and the workplace to compare myself to others. The latter really fed the comparison race. A salesperson is measured only by the last deal they closed and then it's back to ground zero again. I once was a salesperson in the technology industry. The highs and lows of being a salesperson can really take a physical toll on the body, particularly because of the entertaining of clients with food and drinks in order to develop rapport with them. It is what I was taught to do in the hopes of becoming the favoured vendor/supplier. It seems I was constantly trying to be that special one.

One way to get out of the habitual paradigm of comparing oneself to others is to be presented with an opportunity to get out of one's familiar environment.

✳✳✳

To do so, I accepted an invitation to be part of a group adventure to climb Mt. Kilimanjaro to co-celebrate my birthday with a friend as we share the same Leo birth day. Entertaining the idea of climbing a mountain to its 19,340-foot summit was a very scary challenge for me, both mentally and physically. After years of suffering from fibromyalgia and walking with a cane, who was I to think I could attempt such an adventure? My husband was so encouraging; he convinced me that if I trained for it I could do it. As loving as my husband was, this experience would also be a milestone in our marriage of love and trust. I saw that he believed I could physically do this climb. It's the first time I could hear and feel his belief that I could accomplish something that I perceived was so out of reach for me. So I trained, paid for the climb, bought my airline ticket and met 15 women in Moshi, Tanzania in August 2008. I knew only my Leo sister. We spent a couple of days together to get to know each other and to get acclimatized to our new surroundings.

As we trekked up the mountain through the rainforest, I had the opportunity to learn about my fellow climbers as we shared the stories of our lives. At times, I walked in silence taking in unfamiliar foliage and smiling when encountering the tiny orchids on the path. The lead guide, Simon, kept tabs on me and watched my physical health closely, as he knew I suffered from fibromyalgia and asthma. Before embarking on our journey, I turned my two puffer containers over to him. Though they had never met each other, both my family doctor and Simon agreed that Simon would know when I would need my puffer for breathing.

On the second leg of our trek, Simon could see I was having difficulty breathing. He pulled me aside and said, "pole, pole," which is pronounced "polay, polay". It means slowly, slowly in Swahili and so he took out my puffer and administered it for me, so I could breathe. What I didn't realize was how slow I had been walking and that I was no longer hiking with the group. After I had the opportunity to take a few full deep breaths, I looked at Simon with shame because I hadn't kept up. The shame I felt in that moment was similar to the shame I felt for not ever going to university like my high school friends. He sensed my self-inflicted humiliation and, with a big smile, he placed his hand on my shoulder and gently said, "One foot in front of the other, Delane. Don't think of anything else. Just one foot in front of the other; pole pole."

We set off hoping that I would catch up, but I was too far behind. I was mentally beating myself up with sucker punches filled with fear and anger and when it became loud enough for Simon to feel the mental abuse I was inflicting on myself, he'd bring me back to the present moment by placing his large hand on my small shoulder, smiling with the supportive words 'pole, pole'. The sun had run its daily course in the African sky and yearned to stay in the sky long enough to see me back to camp but even the sun cannot change the natural forces. Soon it would be the moon's turn to light my way.

Worry began to set in as I could see the tents far off in the distance. Then exhaustion appeared and the slow movement of my feet told Simon how tired I was. After I noticed the sun was only four inches above the horizon, Simon patted me on the shoulder with exuberance and sang out with joy, "Delane, listen they are singing you to camp!" When I looked up to see what Simon meant, I could see our amazing porters singing and dancing and welcoming all of us to camp. To see such joy accompanied with a symphony of tenors and deep baritone voices was so inspirational.

In my stubbornness, I kept my eyes mostly cast down following the steps of my guide and not one time did I look up to see where I was going! It takes a fool to realize one's folly because it turned out I was only about 150-200 yards behind my fellow trekkers. Simon continued to me by imploring me. "Go, go join your friends!" I too wanted to relieve my back of my backpack and free my hands of the walking poles, so I picked up the pace, staying focused on the men dancing and singing all of us to camp. One by one, each of us set our packs down on the tarp laid out for us and joined them dancing as they sang. Simon, already dancing as we approached camp, took my hand and escorted me to meet the rest. I found the strength to dance with him as I shuffled my feet using the walking sticks as support. He helped me remove my pack from my shoulders and melodically chanted in my ear, "Go, dance."

I joined the group slowly moving my body in a stylized version of the monster mash because I was so fatigued. As we all celebrated that we were together again as one, our troupe of trekkers, porters and trustworthy guides danced until the last bit of sunlight winked at us before turning the sky over to its friend, the moon. We dined and celebrated and then, with a full belly, I nestled into my sleeping bag and welcomed a much needed restful sleep.

On day six, my tent mate and I were greeted with hot tea at 5:00 a.m. in the vestibule of our tent. In a sing-songy voice, our porter chimed, "Good Morning." When I unzipped the entrance of the inner tent, our eyes met and he smiled a big smile proclaiming, 'It's a good day for a climb.' I confidently smiled back with, "Yes, it is!"

The schedule indicated that the day's climb was broken into two parts. The first part of the day we would climb to Lava Tower to stop for lunch and acclimatize our bodies at 15,200 feet. After lunch, the plan was for the group to descend through the Senecio habitat to camp at the base of the Baranco Wall. After breakfast, the morning routine of having our heart rates and blood pressure recorded was checked off. We then filled all of our water vessels; this hike was going to be a long one. The tour company had it marked as a seven to eight-hour trek but something in my gut told me I was not going to make it in the allotted time. I could feel the anxiety beginning to swirl beneath my abdomen, so I took in a slow deep breath while counting to eight, and then exhaled to a count of eight. Doing this several times calmed my nerves. With my pack on, I joined the ladies who were filled with excitement. Lava Tower was to be a sight to see and a significant milestone in our trek.

One of our four guides led the way and we sixteen women were off on the trail. I recall back on Day One when we hiked as one organism. In our group, some women were physically more athletic than others, some liked to photograph along the way to capture every moment and others were just taking the experience in. The variety in our collective precipitated our group of one to break into three smaller groups. When we rested for a snack, we reconnected as one group, but once back on the trail, each person would naturally hike at her own pace, breaking the group back into the three clusters.

Having been on the trail for some time after our brief rest, I noticed the group's voices were disappearing in front of me. In a panic, I turned around and saw Simon right behind me with that familiar smile that brought my anxiety level down though not by much because when I looked in front of me, the ladies were out of sight. I liked the feeling of our group being one organism because of that sense of belonging but I felt that, not seeing them was a metaphor of my life. It reminded me that I was not part of my group of friends who graduated university nor was I part of the family I was born to. My questioning and self-doubt consumed my mind and it was affecting *my body's performance to keep time with my Kili sisters. I continued on knowing that Simon was behind me. He was going to make sure this little soldier put one foot in front of the other, marching through my life, through my days. I just kept soldiering on.*

However, with each step I took I could feel a flood of memories that had been long buried. It felt like someone had fully opened the gates of my emotion and, whoever opened them, did not request my permission.

My thoughts and emotions went back to the time I was twenty-three and my heart belonged to a man who was sixteen years my senior. I was his rebound from a divorce and he was my knight in shining armour after a deceitful four-year relationship. The memories of happy times, making dinners together, sharing moments of laughter and special occasions when his nine-year old son would join us made me feel like we were family. Despite recalling the good, it was overshadowed by one Sunday afternoon where the two of us were dueling it out with words.

❅❅❅

Eli, altitude sickness set in and this skeleton came out of the closet in the form of an internal verbal exchange. It was like watching an ominous storm rolling in from the ocean and there was no mobile weather app to tell me when it would end.

❅❅❅

Filled with frustration and anger, our uncivil, oral battle erupted. With tears streaming down my face, I pleaded to find out what had changed in our relationship. "Everything was fine until I had surgery?! What happened? I don't understand!" He was a formidable six-foot two-inches standing in front of me like a basketball guard who had just stolen the ball from the other team. It felt as though he was coming down the court for the slam dunk as he screamed, "You are no longer a woman to me!" The shock of hearing those words silenced me because just three weeks before I had to undergo a complete hysterectomy with bilateral salpingo-oophorectomy due to suffering from several years of severe endometriosis.

The inner me retreated into the cave deep within my soul and was processing his words. The lion, my outer self, roared back, "Explain yourself!" His face was beet red as he blurted, 'You have no ovaries and no uterus! You're not a woman!' The vibration of his words forever imprinted themselves into every cell of my being. In my stoic silence, I picked up all the broken pieces of myself that were lying shattered on the floral print sofa and the Indigenous hand-woven rug. Taking in a deep breath, while counting to five, I exhaled so that I could refrain from picking something up off the coffee table and throwing it at him. When my four-foot eleven inch being walked by him to leave, I held my head high, looked up at him to meet his eyes and stated, "I am a woman."

Simon interrupted the flowing river of the past with his admonition, "Delane, Delane. Drink some water. You have not had water in the last 15 minutes.' Heeding his order, I grabbed the hose off my shoulder and sucked the water out of the bladder in my pack. In that moment, I felt the water cleansing my body of the hurt and shame of feeling less than a woman.

With his encouraging hand on my shoulder, Simon asked, "How are you feeling?"

In that moment, I was actually feeling good and supported my word by giving him a nod. We kept moving along the trail until I saw a tall rock. Suddenly I felt I needed to lean against it using my hands to steady myself. Suddenly I had the spins and like a broken piñata dispensing all of its colourful treasures I did the same except my contents were not treasures; it was breakfast. Altitude sickness announced that it was fully in charge of my body and I needed to pay attention. My trek to Lava Tower became the new HIIT workout for me. I'm not talking about High Intensity Interval Training rather High Intensity Interval Therapy, because my routine now alternated between emptying this mammalian vessel of its negativity, whether solid or energetic matter and placing one foot in front of the other as I recounted every traumatic event that happened to me.

At one point, I remember saying out loud to myself, "Pole, pole; slowly, slowly."

As I continued, my mind continued to wander into the rabbit hole of my soul, where I fell into a black, cavernous void surrounded by traumatic memories of mental and sexual abuse by another boyfriend. There were more snapshots of gut wrenching pain before my eyes as I recounted numerous relationships of perceived love lost.

Since I was a child, the vault in my soul catalogued the varying degrees of hurt where no Dewey decimal system was needed. Each record of hurt took over geographic areas of my body from the corner of my elbow to the whole southern hemisphere below by rib cage. There comes a time when the body has no vacancy for smiles, happiness or an inkling of love. Illness seizes the opportunity to orchestrate a perfect storm on the body. After months of lacking mental and physical energy, I was diagnosed with fibromyalgia. There were bed-ridden days, weeks on end of depression and worse, the admission of physical defeat and the humiliating experience of walking with a cane at the age of thirty.

I retreated into silence once again embarrassed that I could not 'hold it together' physically and for allowing the ghost of altitude sickness take over my body. As I recounted one tragedy after another, the weight of my body got heavier despite forging ahead with Simon at my side. As the air got thinner with less oxygen my story-telling filter was absent from the mind and soul. I was not aware that I had shared some of the most horrific Tatay stories with Simon. Little salty soldiers had been streaming down my face for quite some time and the weight of the salt was like invisible weights pulling me down to the ground. They finally sent me to my knees with hands catching my fall then gripping the sand and gravel in my palms, crying with a piercing yell, 'Why, Simon, why?! Why would he do that to me?' If someone had passed by they would have thought that Simon became my God as I buried my forehead into the rocky earth wanting to feel physical pain.

The thud of a backpack hitting the ground behind me was heard. Simon was at my side on the ground. With empathy he offered, "I don't know why, Delane, but he is not here now. Kilimanjaro's Summit is waiting for you, my sister." As if by some magic, the tears receded and my breathing slowed aware now that I needed oxygen. I knew he was right. I was allowing my past to hinder the present and the incredible opportunity to make the summit. It was in this moment I felt shame once again for acting like such a child and a fool by allowing my memories to affect my present. The only person that I was holding back was me.

Still on my knees, I pushed myself up to see the sun and I brushed the bits of sand and tiny rocks off my face. Like a great boxing coach, Simon offered his hand to pull me up . I took his hand and together we got me back on my feet. Pulling the cap off the water hose, I took in a cool sip of water, which cleansed the fine dust in my mouth and throat. Simon instructed me to not speak and to stay focused on breathing because of the altitude we were at. I needed oxygen. He let me know, in no uncertain terms that, if I didn't heed his advice he was going to send me down the mountain. Together we walked in silence for what seemed like another 15 minutes and I had thought I was doing fine until I fell to my knees again.

Simon helped me to a nearby rock to sit on. This time there were no words of encouragement, "Delane, sit and wait." I started crying again but this time my tears were out of fear. Fear that he was sending me down. My fifteen minutes of hope in thinking I could make it to the summit were dashed by the prospect of waiting for the other guides to take me down.

With a hint of frustration in his voice he asked, 'Why are you crying again, my sister?'

Since the rock I was sitting on was only six inches off the ground, I looked up at him and admitted, "Because you're sending me down."

The shame of being sent down the mountain was one thing but to think that I was going to go home and tell my husband that all the training I did and his belief in me wasn't enough for me to make the summit would be another failure feather in my cap. Defeated, I crossed my arms, placed them on my knees as a resting spot for my forehead. With my eyes closed, footsteps could be heard and my heart sank.

Three sets of feet could be seen to the right under my elbow. When I looked up, Simon handed me an avocado sandwich and with a smile, encouraged me to eat. With one bite left of my sandwich, he unwrapped a corn fritter and said, 'Eat.' My stomach was full and I didn't want to eat another bite. Paying no attention to my protest, he said again, "Eat." Not wanting to cross Simon I started into the corn fritter imagining it was filled with ice cream in the hopes that it would slide down my throat easily. The latter trick didn't work. Half way through I was having a hard time swallowing and stopped eating. He was having none of it and directed me to drink the chamomile tea out of the thermos and continue eating. Opposing his directive, I clamored, 'I can't. It feels like I'm swallowing sand!' Then he calmly said, "We are not moving until you eat that fritter and the boiled egg they brought you. You are going to eat.'"

In this moment, I was reminded of the time when I was seven years old and told to eat the liver on my plate by Tatay's friend. It didn't matter that I didn't want to eat the flat, leathery grey thing called food. The man slammed his hand on the dining table and demanded that I finish everything on my plate including the liver. Tatay's friend was six foot, five inches and I was afraid of him, so I did what I was told and ate my meal as tears streamed onto my plate without a whimper heard.

Beads of wet salt streamed from my eyes and down my face. I chewed, swallowed and took in a sip of tea to get the fritter down. I was being sent down the mountain anyway, so I did as I was told. The tears stopped as I took a bite of the boiled egg. Now that I was out of the vault of pain, I looked around and took in the beautiful landscape coming to terms with this present moment as my version of the summit. Taking in a deep breath, I accepted being sent down and I finished the boiled egg. I drank the last bit of tea in the thermos and asked Simon, "Who am I going down with?" He chuckled while the other guide along with the other two porters smiled. Simon, cheerfully said, "Come on get up! Let's go join your Kili sisters!"

"I'm not being sent down?" I wanted to make sure I fully understood what was going on and to confirm I was not in another delirious state. "No, you need to make it to Lava Tower and eat more food. You've been burning more calories than you've been taking in that's why I made you eat all that food," he said with a smile. Without missing a beat Simon continued on with, "Come, sister, let's go."

My small goal was to make it to Lava Tower and eat more food. If I could do that and keep Ego from opening the cave of demons again, the prospect of making it to the top of Mt. Kilimanjaro was in my sights!

Simon was right. I wasn't taking in enough food, so we agreed that, even if I thought I was full, I would eat another bowl or two of stew, have three to four sandwiches and snack on nuts or eat half sandwiches more often. With this new tactic, I was able to leave Lava Tower Camp and make it to Crater Camp with the group. When we were in the crater, there was enough light for Simon to point out how we would make our way to the top. For me, going up a wall of scree seemed scarier than going up the Baranco Wall. I was told that this part of the climb is difficult because when you take one step forward, your leg gets swallowed in by tiny lava rock, making the next step difficult. Having never done a hike like this before I imagined that I would be thigh deep in small volcanic rock which suggested that this would be the most difficult part of my climb since experiencing altitude sickness prior to Lava Tower. Later that evening, after dinner and medical check-ins,

I retreated to the comfort of my sleeping bag and meditated. This lulled me into slumber.

After a restful sleep, the morning was jump started by the warm smile of our porter as we were greeted with hot chamomile tea and honey. We all gathered in the mess tent for breakfast and medical check-ins followed by a pep talk that included tactics for going up to the summit. Embracing this sense of empowerment was a new feeling for me and I was relishing it! I was so excited for this part of the journey! Once again, Simon was by my side sharing words of encouragement that inspired me to keep going and not look back. I stayed focus on the words pole pole 'slowly slowly,' placing one foot in front of the other. The scree lived up to its challenge but fortunately each step did not sink into the loose rock as deep as I had anticipated; it only came up to my knee. With each step I was careful to watch my breathing ensuring I was taking full breaths not short, shallow ones. Breathing helped me stay focused safeguarding the cave of demons in my soul to remain closed. When I looked up I could see the ridge getting closer prompting Simon to whisper, "You're almost there. Keep going." With his words in my ears, it was eight more steep steps and I was on the ridge. Euphoria filled me as I took in the sky, clouds and the incredible feeling that I was on top of the earth. With tears of joy, I gave Simon a hug of gratitude and asked him, "Did I really make it to the top?" He patted me on the head like a big brother does to his little sister as he replied, "You made it to the top of the ridge! The peak is there where the sign is! Go, you're almost there, Delane!"

I, along with several Kili Sisters, made it to Uruhu Peak. Our achievement was documented with individual and group shots taken in front of the crooked, weathered sign stating Congratulations | Uruhu Peak Tanzania 5,895m/19,340ft.

As I waited for the others to have their photos taken, I looked out past the imposing large ice mass and all there was before me was beautiful blue sky. This sky bore witness to all that happened on the mountain; the very same sky that bore witness to my life in another part of the world. It was in this moment that my heart filled with gratitude because I realized that the sky witnessed me making it to the summit just as it had observed me living through my traumas. If the sky can witness the good and the bad that have happened to me, couldn't I do the same for myself? Must all my memories *be ones of pain? Then it occurred to me, it took climbing a mountain to realize that I was worthy of experiencing good but how can that be? The Delane album cover had always been titled 'Bad Person' with Songs of Shame, Pain and Darkness in the genre of Trauma.*

Then I remembered I chose to put one foot in front of the other to make it to Lava Tower. Because of that choice I was standing on the summit of Mt. Kilimanjaro feeling on top of the world! I realized that I neglected to give myself the gift of Choice. Instead, I chose to stay stuck in the story I played over and over again since I was a child instead of choosing to grow. I've been depriving myself of growing! Whoa!!! I soaked in this realization in silence for a few more moments then brought both hands over my heart as an expression of love to myself for the first time as an adult. With eyes closed I whispered into the wind, "Thank you, Kili' and I smiled.

✳✳✳

Did I need to climb Mt. Kilimanjaro to learn that it was me holding me back, Eli? Who is to say maybe yes, maybe no but this experience was an important milestone in my life. Maybe I needed to go elsewhere where nothing was familiar in order for me to 'see' that I deserved happiness, joy and love. It's not until I pushed beyond the self-imposed boundaries built out of fear that I discovered who I am capable of being.

Well, Eli, I think I took you through an interesting journey in this letter, so I'll let you sit with it and will be in touch sometime soon.

With much gratitude for listening,

Delane

Love is a fruit in season at all times, and within reach of every hand.
– Mother Teresa

CHAPTER 7: GIVE LOVE

Dear Eli,

Today is Wednesday and I'm heading back home. I am grateful that the train was on time, so I could start writing to you. I picked up some new stationary downstairs in the concourse. Though there are rows of different colours to choose from I continue to select variable whites with no lines. Why complicate reading my letters with a coloured background when my printing may be difficult to read since it's so artsy.

The train is filled with many families going to Montreal. It's interesting to watch kids who are naturally curious to see if there are other children on the train. Like gophers popping their heads out of the ground, little ones stand on their seats or on top of the laps of their parents to peer above the field of heads and seatbacks to see if they can spot other child comrades. The four-year-old boy in 12B initiated a wave hello to a girl of similar age in 9D and the two of them have been giggling during their ongoing exchange. The young flirters were interrupted when the boy's mother commanded him to sit down. Disappointed that her new friend was no longer visible, she disappeared into her designated hole landing on her seat.

The number of families on this train suggests that many commuters might be on holiday possibly making this ride home a boisterous one.

As more people were shuffling into the train car, I noticed something shiny catch my eye. Light was reflecting off the gold ribbons from the many gifts that were bursting out of a bag a lady was carrying. Behind her were children obeying orders to follow her and a man carrying another two bags with even more gifts. The man, woman and children walked passed me to their seats located in the back of the car taking up the last two rows of four seaters facing each other. Either they were attending an incredible celebration or maybe one of the family members in their troupe had cause to be celebrated by the number of gifts brought on board.

Seeing the bag of gifts set off a string of memories that brought me back to a time in my mid-twenties. With headphones on, chamomile tea at my side and pen and paper out, I'm ready to share the story of how a phone call brought calm to this young adult during a time when I was going through my own internal dark storm.

Similar to previous letters, I need to lay the foundation of the importance of this phone call.

❋❋❋

So please allow me to take you back to the beginning, a time in high school when I attended a Friday night house party. There I met a new friend, Kristen. She had heard through a mutual friend that I slept in the locomotive train at the park the night before. Under the night sky with stars twinkling above , we sat in the corner of the backyard amongst the bamboo. With red plastic cups in hand, full of beer fresh from the keg, she patiently listened as I gave her the abridged version of my life. When I was finished, I took a long sip of my beer and cast my eyes down into the blackness of the soil beneath us. Kristen placed her crimson cup beside her and held my face in her hands and said, "Tonight, you'll sleep at my house." Her generosity was bigger than my ego so without any hesitation, I took her up on her offer. The idea of sleeping again on a cold steel train bench without a blanket was the least comfortable option despite the train being a place of safety in my dreams. That night was the first night I slept through the night in seven years.

The next morning Kristen asked that I stay upstairs in her bedroom while she spoke to her mom. She explained that I was going through a difficult time with family and asked if I could stay the weekend. With empathy, her mom agreed. She asked Kristen to bring me downstairs to meet them. Footsteps made their way up the stairs and Kristen said, "It's cool. They want to meet you." I got up from the loveseat in her room and followed her like a good soldier out of the bedroom, into the hallway and down the stairs. As we walked through the living room towards the dining room, a man and a woman were seated at the table. Nervous, I could feel my heart racing as my body filled with anxiety. We weren't quite in the dining room yet and Kristen introduced me, "This is Delane." I looked at them and felt like a deer in headlights.

Following Kristen's introduction, Judy spoke up and said, "Hi, I'm Judy. This is Bill." The room filled with an awkward silence for a moment then Judy inquired, "Do you speak?" I chuckled replying, 'Yes.' With relief she laughed and pronounced, "Good. Nice to meet you. Kristen says that you'll be spending time here over the weekend. We have to go out for dinner tonight. Maybe we'll see you two for breakfast tomorrow."

Kristen thanked her mom and the two of us were off to meet one of Kristen's friends.

On Monday while Judy was at work, Kristen and I were at school trying to figure out a plan for me to stay for the rest of the week since her mom was going away on holiday. For two teenagers, our plan seemed simple. Kristen would call her mom at work, ask for permission over the phone and her mom would agree. As per the plan, Kristen made the call but there was one hitch. Before Judy would agree to me staying at their house, Judy wanted to meet my parents. Kristen said she'd call her back. When Kristen asked me what we should do I replied, "Well, I have a social worker, so she could meet your mom." After making the arrangements on my end with the social worker to meet with Judy, Kristen called her mom back. "Mom, Delane doesn't have parents but she has a social worker. Please be at the house at 3:30 p.m. to meet her." Not waiting for a response from her mom, Kristen hung up the phone.

3:30 p.m. came and the meeting took place in the same dining room where I met Judy and Bill two days prior. It was agreed that I could stay for the week. The seven days turned into weeks and weeks into months. Before we knew it, I was celebrating my first Christmas with Kristen and her family. Not to be left out of the family celebration, Judy stitched my name on a Christmas stocking and hung it with the other stockings on the mantle. For the Christmas holidays that followed, Bill and Judy opened their hearts and included me as one of their own.

✳✳✳

Eli, you have no idea how full my heart felt to be part of a family where it was safe to sleep at night.

✳✳✳

Though I had this refuge, it didn't take away the memories of what happened to me in the past and I found myself testing the boundaries with Judy and Bill because I believed I was damaged goods. I endeavoured to give them reason to not want anything to do with me. It all came to a head when Judy announced that her mission would be for me to graduate from high school. It didn't matter that I didn't want to get up for school; she was there to whip back the blankets, spray me with cold water to get me up and take me to school. Her tenacity and belief in me paid off because I did graduate. As more Christmas holidays were ticked off the calendar, Kristen's family became my family. Judy and Bill became my guardians yet, unbeknownst to them, I cast them in the role of parents in my life's movie.

Then one Christmas, I was too embarrassed to see them. I was on the brink of losing my job and my self-esteem was very low. Consequently, flashbacks of abuse and confusion consumed my mind. My highs and lows were like a marine ship in the open ocean sitting on the crest of a monster wave going for a nosedive. There didn't seem to be any relief from the storm and I was sinking. How I yearned for a dead calm.

Knowing I had to make the Christmas phone call to wish them happy holidays, I was shamefaced by the fact I did not even have the decency to send them a small gift or card. I didn't see how I could pull myself together from the depression I was in. Wanting to put on a brave voice for the call, I felt a walk was called for. The cool air caressed my face as if it were calling me to be present and inviting me to feel the hardness of the cement below my feet, to hear the leaves rustling in the wind and to see the numerous shades of grey in the sky in contrast to the various greens amongst the grass and trees. Getting out of my head became more and more difficult during this time but walks were an easy, accessible remedy. The further I walked, the more the happier times came into my mind's eye. I remembered the time when I came home from school and Judy told me to go upstairs to her room. There on her bed was a closed green garbage bag tied with curled ribbons of pink and yellow. Taped onto the bag was an envelope. When

I opened it, it read 'Kristen has her teddy bear to sleep with at night. You should have an animal to sleep with too. Hope you like him.' I opened the garbage bag revealing a black and white plush penguin wearing a winter red knit hat topped with a white pom-pom and matching sweater with snowflakes on it. I scooped him up into my arms and hugged him like a two-year-old, not a fifteen-year-old. From that moment forward, I sought comfort with Pengy in my arms; I no longer hugged myself curled up in a ball at the bottom of the bathroom tub rocking back and forth crying myself to sleep. Pengy became my buddy and lifeline when Judy wasn't around to hear all my troubles. As I continued to walk, this memory brought a smile to my face and love to my heart.

The cold wind encouraged me to continue on my jaunt. With hands in my coat pocket, I moved forward with no intended destination putting one foot in front of the other. Then a memory of Bill came when I was seventeen. It was a Friday night two weeks before Christmas. He said, "Hey, Kid, get your coat on. I need to get Judy a Christmas present."

Not questioning him, I grabbed my coat and off to the department store we went. Like most big store layouts, the make-up and fragrance counters were lined up, one after another. Bill knew where he was going, so I followed passing the various harmonious and sometimes vile scents called fragrance. He stopped at the Estee Lauder counter and motioned me to join him at the counter. He caught the eye of the cosmetic salesperson that asked, "Can I help you?" As he pointed to me, Bill replied, "Yes. Can you do her face up?"

One of the many facets I appreciated and feared about Bill was his bluntness with words. I don't know if being blunt came with being an artisan plasterer, but I felt safe around him. The salesperson agreed and invited me to sit up on the stool in front of the counter. Having never had the experience of make-up being applied professionally, I could hardly contain my excitement and wondered if I would look any different. As she cleansed my face and applied a light foundation, we engaged in small talk about my age and make-up experience. I don't recall how long I sat in the chair but when she was finished, she turned to Bill asking, "So what do you think?" Smiling he asked me, "What do you think?" When I turned towards the mirror, I couldn't believe my eyes. The person in the mirror was pretty. Were we the same person? Bill asked again, "So?"

In disbelief that I was actually looking at myself, I replied, "Wow, makeup makes me look different." Curious the sales clerk asked, "Different in a good way?" I answered by nodding my head indicating yes. Then Bill turned to the salesperson and said, "Everything you put on her face, I will buy." The purchase happened so fast and the next thing I knew I was holding an Estee Lauder bag filled with make-up. We thanked the staff for their help and as we left the counter. I turned to Bill and hugged him saying, "Thank you." His reply was simply, "No problem, kid."

It turned out that we weren't out to go shopping for Judy. He used that as a hook for me to go with him to the department store. My heart smiled again when I remembered Judy telling me that someone described Bill as a steel-clad teddy bear with a heart of gold. Whoever came up with the description nailed Bill to a tee.

The temperature was dropping so I made my way back to the place where I was living at the time. I zipped my jacket up to the neckline and made a conscious effort to recall more joyful memories so as not to let my spirit fall prey to the grey sky. When I reached the apartment, I removed my shoes and went to the kitchen to warm the kettle for a cup of tea. When the kettle whistle blew, I turned the burner off, poured water into the mug dousing the tea bag and brought the mug to the counter where the phone was mounted on the wall. I took a deep inhale in, picked up the phone and asked the operator to help me place a collect call to the place where my happier memories were born.

When Judy accepted the collect call, I mustered up as much positivity as I could and said, "Merry Christmas, Judy".

I pictured her smiling and happy that I called, even though it was collect. "Merry Christmas! How are you?"

Though my words did not match how I felt inside, I answered, "Ok...kind of but not really. I mean I may lose my job, but I have an interview next week, so we'll see."

"Well, let us know how the interview goes. Ok? Oh, did you get the Christmas card that Bill and I sent you?"

'Yes, I did.' I paused for a moment to take a sip of tea then continued with, "Judy, I'm really sorry I didn't send you and Bill a card or gift. It's been a bit tough lately."

"That's ok, Honey."

"No, it's not ok but there is one gift I'd like to give you. It's the only gift I can come up with and it would mean the world to me if you were open to accepting it."

"Ok. What is it?" her curiosity piqued.

Tears welled up as I hoped the words would be appropriately expressed. "Judy, you and Bill have done so much for me and I know I could never repay you for everything you've given me. The only thing I can give you is… is the gift to call you Mom and Dad.' As the tears salted my face, I went on "My parents didn't earn the right to be called mom and dad, but you and Bill have so can I call you Mom and Dad? There I said it."

Without hesitation, she said, "Yes. Yes, you may call us Mom and Dad. It would be an honour for us to be your parents."

"Merry Christmas, Mom! Thank you for making me feel like I belong to a real family. You'll tell Bill then that he's my Dad, right?" The tears were of joy because I no longer wanted to refer to them as my guardians. I wanted them as my Mom and Dad.

"Yes, I'll tell Bill that you'll be calling him Dad from now on. You know we love you?"

"Yes, Mom."

I was overcome with feeling a sense of calm that instantly softened the emotional stormy waves I had been experiencing. I offered to let her go since she had family and friends over at the house. I promised that I would call her next week and with that I returned the receiver to the phone's cradle.

✻✻✻

Eli, to this day Judy is my mom and Kristen, my sister. My dad passed away in 2001 but there isn't a day that goes by when he is not in my thoughts. Whenever I enter or leave my house, mom and dad's photo is either the first thing or last thing I see.

Looking back as I am writing this letter to you, I framed that call as if it was I giving Judy and Bill the gift of calling them my parents. I believe I needed to call them mom and dad, so I had someone to hold onto to call my family. I had felt lost and alone for so long that I needed to feel that I belonged to a family, one that I love very much. And you know what, Eli? I know they love me.

I am grateful for the family who came on board the train with all those gifts, so I could share with you the love I have for my family. Believe it or not the train is not as boisterous as I had thought early on. Many of the children are napping or playing video games.

Seeing I still have fifteen more minutes before arrival, I'll pen a quick note to my sister.

In gratitude for listening and hope to meet one day soon,

Delane

It is sometimes difficult to view compassion and loving kindness as the strengths they are.
– Sharon Salzberg

CHAPTER 8: GRANDMA

Dear Eli,

This morning I pulled out my sketchbook to design a new ring, but got distracted by the golden sunrays showering on the green farm fields. Freight train traffic forced our early morning commuter train to stop and go like an inchworm moving forward with no set schedule. At one pause on our journey, I noticed one weed standing alone in the rows of alfalfa. I'm horrible at identifying plants outside of the simple dandelion or milkweed but I thought this lone weed looked beautiful amongst the manicured farm field. I thought it was a shame that the field would most likely be sprayed with an herbicide to kill what did not belong amongst the rest of the vegetation. The service manager apologized for our delay into Toronto notifying us that we would be 20 minutes late and with that the train continued. When we stopped at our scheduled Cobourg station, a passenger boarded and walked by towards her unassigned seat. Suddenly, the scent of her perfume halted the streaming ideas for my new ring design. I recognized the scent of my grandmother and I was compelled to pull out my laptop to share this memory with you.

※※※

I idolized my grandmother. She was a Filipina immigrant from Leyte. My grandparents came over from the Philippines after WWII. Their family had 12 children. Grandma was teacher, cook and seamstress who always seemed to be filled with laughter and love. While raising children and sewing, she went back to school to finish grade eight, obtain her high school diploma and graduate from university at the age of 56. I cherished my summers as a child, since I spent most of my time with her learning how to sew. Sewing was in her blood. Scissors, needle and thread were extensions of her arms. She knew how to use another tool that non-sewers would overlook as important – the iron. For a seamstress, the iron flattens wrinkled fabric that freshly came from the fabric store, a fabric remnant or an article of clothing that needed repair. The iron is the invisible assistant when prepping for a hem, creating darts or pleats and fusing interface, which stiffens the fabric, for shirt collars and cuffs so the fabric can easily glide through the sewing machine to accomplish a perfect seam.

※※※

Today, as a goldsmith, I use the flame of a torch and solder to connect metals together.

※※※

The sewing machine was her means of connecting patterns of fabric together as well as connecting her to people whether they be family members, students of the city college, the priest from the church or the local parishioners.

An outdoor porch was converted into Grandma's sewing room that was 7' x15' long and this was where she held court. Squabbles between her kids were settled while she was in front of the sewing machine. All the problems of the world could be solved at the sewing machine as far as my grandmother was concerned. However, it was also where I once saw my grandmother break down and cry.

One summer evening, while on the floor cutting out a pattern for a new skirt, I asked about her family. She was at the sewing machine repairing trousers for the local high school football team. As she spoke, the sewing machine's needle pierced the material in a non-rhythmic pace. By seeing her foot inconsistently depress the pedal of the machine, I could feel the expressed emotional pain of her story.

She was 18 when she ran through the jungle with three children escaping the bombing of the Japanese. She had a one-year old daughter and her sister's twin sons. She and her sister had to flee their home or they would have been killed. While in the jungle, her sister died shortly after giving birth to the twin boys. She was alive long enough to name them and then her spirit left her body before my Grandma's eyes. There was no time for Grandma to bury her sister since a bomb dropped and exploded somewhere nearby. She scooped up the three children and ran. The tears started streaming down Grandma's face when she told me that there was no time to bury her own sister. The quiver in her voice expressed the guilt she felt leaving her sister there in the open to rot and have her body exposed to the animals and insects. Grandma stopped the sewing machine and wiped her tears with the cuff of her housecoat. As she picked up another pair of trousers, she continued to tell me that she had to nurse all three children. Soon her body no longer produced milk for lack of food; one of the twins died. Once again, there was no time to bury this little baby named Mario and she set him under a tree and then ran with her daughter and now a baby boy she would mother as her own.

The sewing machine stopped. Her hands cupped her tiny face as the tears bled through her tired calloused hands. The words that cut that summer evening air were, "They never helped me. They never helped me. They never helped me." At 10 years old, I got up from the floor and placed my hand on her back as she sobbed. I also never asked who "they" were.

I will never forget that evening. It is the kind of memory that resides in three places – my mind, my body and my heart. My mind holds the image of a small framed 4' 8" woman, dwarfed even more by wearing a 100-pound cloak of guilt and shame. My body wanted to hug my grandmother, but I didn't for I also feared her. Over the years, my heart grew to appreciate the pain and suffering my grandmother experienced for I know nothing about running from bombs, surviving in a jungle with children nor leaving the dead without proper closure. I acknowledge I live in a western world where I am able to travel by car, train or plane, afford a root over my head and attend celebrations of life with friends and family. Yes, I know nothing of her pain.

Eli, I am ashamed to admit the following story to you of my grandmother. As you can see from what I just shared, my grandmother should be revered but as an adult it can be exhausting in the areas of conscious forgiveness despite my admiration and compartmentalized love for her.

This is my story of complicated love for a female/mother figure whom I cherished. Eli, this time I need to take you back to when I was 15 years old. It was the day I had filed my report with the police. On that particular day,

I was staying at the home of a family friend and I received a phone call. I picked up the landline and took it into my room as the phone chord trailed behind me.

"Hello?" I said in an inquisitive voice. "This is Grandma" was all I could hear.

On the inside, it felt as if a large giant came by and showered me with a noxious spray of fear like an herbicide trying to kill any vegetation in its path. It entered into my bloodstream causing my stomach to feel nauseous. My breath became shallow, palms sweaty and the roots beneath my feet seemed to retreat back into my body for the only oxygen available was within me. Fear has no light. Fear turns black. On the outside, my 15-year-old body wanted a hug like a wild flower being caressed by a breeze or the feeling of being needed by a visiting monarch butterfly. But, on the inside, I was cold as I could feel the imagined darkness that was about to descend on me.

"Hi Grandma."

"You put your father in jail. How could you do this to him? I'm going to get him out," She said with the fierceness of a mother lion.

"You can't do that Grandma."

"Yes, I can and I will."

"Do you know what he did Grandma?"

The landline phone could not handle the magnitude of decibels coming from the other side as the chilling words a child never wants to hear from their own grandmother were, "They told me what you said. You must have enticed your father. You must have been prancing around the house in slinky pajamas. Yes, that's what you did. Isn't it? That's what you did! What do you have to say for yourself?! This is your Grandma – ANSWER me!"

I felt paralyzed and I had no way of responding immediately. How could she not believe me? She's my Grandma. I loved her and I know she loved me. In the space of three seconds, my mind and heart were flooded with so many memories of hugs before I fell asleep, times at the airport, her pride when I finished a sewing project, the times of pattern and fabric shopping together where agreeing or disagreeing on fabric types was our own secret biathlon, the moments of shared laughter when I incorrectly sewed patterns together and had to rip them part stitch by stitch . They were our sacraments of sewing together. I remembered the countless "I love you's" when I arrived at the beginning of summer or over the phone, as I told her how I was doing at school.

"I said ANSWER me!" demanded Grandma.

By her command, the words came from deep inside me where there is an ocean of feelings that are not shored by any beach. I cried into the receiver. "Ask your son! Ask your son how he could touch his only daughter! Ask your son why he did this to me, your granddaughter! Ask him! Not me!"

It is interesting how my herbicide of fear acted in stages and as such my fear turned into anger. As soon as I said the words "Not me!" the hot molten lava of tears streamed down my cheeks adding a layer of salt on my face. I cried like no 15-year-old child should ever have to cry. A sword of sin pierced my heart and soul by the tongue of my own grandmother. I fell to my knees on the floor, dropping the phone. As the tears fled down my face like the little soldiers obeying orders from some unknown commander to run over a hill because they were told to do so. I wrapped my arms around myself rocking my body to and fro as I attempted to console the child who belonged to no one. Rocking and crying; rocking and crying.

No one came to my room to hug this precious little flower who told the truth and so I resolved, at that moment, never to speak to my grandmother again. It felt like a large boulder rolled in front of an imaginary cave to seal off any love I had for her. My heart would not be open to her after that phone call for there would be no Lazerus moment between us. My tiny body writhed in pain on the floor exhausting every limb while the energy of truth left me evaporating into the ether. This flower may have fallen to the ground, but the writhing shook off the seeds of truth into the soil's universe and I vowed to bloom once again. I awoke the next morning. I did not die.

✳✳✳

Eli, please share if you've ever cried about a loved one like that. Knowing so would provide my heart some comfort in my aloneness. As I write this to you, I realize it's the first time I shared this experience by written word, not by the spoken word. To see the words on paper, bring the uncomfortable duality of shame and empathy. Shame because my grandmother was only doing what a mother would do which is protect her son regardless if the victim was his daughter. Empathy because my grandmother was only doing what a mother would do which is protect her son regardless if the victim was his daughter.

As I sit here on our delayed train to Toronto, I realize that a child remembers love and that kind of love does not die easily especially the love I had for my grandmother. Now as I reflect I can clearly see that forgiveness comes in stages, which was the case with my grandma and me.

✳✳✳

Many years after that phone call, my aunt thought that it would be good for both my grandmother and me to make up, since this frail old lady was starting to exhibit signs of dementia. I never spoke to my aunt about it, but I suppose she wanted her mother to have some peace or closure on this subject of her son and I was the actor cast in the role to forgive.

Aunt Vicki arranged to have grandma come for a visit for several days. I was told the day before. I was staying with my aunt to get back on my feet. I was 24. My grade school and high school friends were holding jobs, living on their own and enjoying the fruits of life that it has to offer to young go-getters in their 20s. I, on the other hand, was lost like a broken sailboat at sea with no mast or rudder. The unsolicited game of comparison came knocking on my door every day to make sure I knew my place. Who was I to think I could amount to anything since I did not go to university? Who was I to think that I could ever be with a man who loved me because the model of a man that resided in every cell of my being was of the one who fathered and invaded me. Some friends from school were in serious relationships and the prospect of them marrying each other was likely. Like a weed, I didn't feel that I belonged in the field of intimate relationships nor the green, grassy meadow of a career.

As I sat at the dining table waiting for my grandmother to arrive from the airport, I was a weed wanting to blossom, but the herbicide of fear showered down once again by the invisible giant in my mind. While I waited, my journal was sitting in front of me and I nervously held my pen in hand. Words did not come to me. As I stared at the journal, the lines seemed to disappear and the molecules of the paper opened up to reveal the image of that painful night years ago after the phone call with Grandma. It was as if I was looking through a kaleidoscope. I saw the many broken pieces of my life creating a colourful image of pain yet, in that pain, I could see the beauty in what happened that night. My grandma, who I dearly loved, was the second female to choose my father over me. It was a scene that could have been written for a theatrical tragedy – except it was real. The beauty that came out was the realization that my grandmother was only protecting her son; the same boy she saved back in the jungle in the Philippines.

When the door opened into the foyer, the sound of footsteps could be heard followed by the hint of conversation as they made their way down the stairs into the open concept kitchen-dining area. As they got closer, the kaleidoscope image of the past disappeared when I closed my journal.

As if it was supposed to be a pleasant surprise for me, Aunt Vicki exclaimed in her upbeat, hopeful voice, "Oh, there you are! Grandma's here!" Her arm was slowly moving up and down presenting Grandma like Vanna White would present a prize on Wheel of Fortune.

I did not get up from the table to greet Grandma and I admit it was disrespectful. Grandma took the seat next to me prompting Aunt Vicki to say, "Well, I'll leave the two of you alone, so you can catch up. It's been such a long time."

Grandma and I sat in silence waiting to see who would say something first. We sat side by side and I stared straight ahead looking at the kitchen cabinets following the wood grain as a means to help me escape from the situation I found myself in. I couldn't bring myself to sit and face Grandma because the feelings of guilt, shame and anger were stirring inside me. The sound of silence was not common between us when I was younger. When we did communicate, there was always the sound of an iron steaming, scissors cutting or the hum of the sewing machine between us. Whether it was mechanical or human, there was always some kind of noise buzzing around us. Then I heard her elbows come down on the dining table as her hands held her crying face. I turned and asked, "Are you ok Grandma?"

She sobbed for the both of us as there were no tears left in me to shed. The memory of watching her cry all those years ago in her sewing room came back to me in an instant. We didn't travel back in time. We were in the present. Years had passed and once again I cautiously placed my hand on her shoulder to offer comfort as I said, "It'll be ok, Grandma. It'll be ok."

The woman I once knew as a force to be reckoned with was here beside me as an old tired soul. This time the guttural crying came from her. In between the deep gasps for air, while tears salted her face and cascaded onto the dining table, came the words, "I'm sorry. I'm so sorry." Her words of apology shocked my heart into a state of both gratitude and shame. Never had I witnessed nor heard from another family member anything close to an apology. The gift of those words was the first step of forgiveness for me. Similar to walking through a labyrinth, forgiveness can help us out of pain or allow us to be stuck and feel trapped rendering the wanderer confused. My grandmother's little 4'8" body looked like she'd been carrying a millstone around her neck for many years. The curve of her back was not because of the osteoporosis but the shackles of pain and regret pinching vertebrae to vertebrae revealing the back of someone who had carried a lifetime of burden.

At the time, a heavy cloak of shame gently landed on my shoulders as I heard her cry. How could I do this to my grandmother? To see her so broken reminded me that I was not the good Catholic I was taught to be. God comes first, my neighbour second and I come third. The gift of 'I'm sorry' was selfish because I had put myself before my grandmother.

✳✳✳

Today, I see that experience very differently. It is a gift I cherish. My grandmother taught me compassion and she helped me to understand that we can forgive and ask for forgiveness at any age.

My train is pulling into Toronto, so I must go. I hope, Eli, one day you'll want to come over and see the quilt that Grandma made as it is draped over one side of my sofa. It was stitched by hand. I think you'd like to see the colours of love, anger and forgiveness.

In gratitude for listening,

Delane

Life is measured in love and positive contributions and moments of grace.
– Carly Fiorina

CHAPTER 9: THE PHONE CALL

Dear Eli,

I'm distracted by the train noise and cannot take a nap, so I need something else to focus on versus the rhythmic sound of the wheels on the rails. Hence, I am writing another letter to you.

Have you ever done something, Eli, and thought afterwards about whether or not you put your best foot forward in that moment? I can tell you I've done my fair share of not putting my best foot forward. When I reflect on why, the honest answer is that I don't know why. It could be stupidity; failing to see a situation for what it was; allowing my ego to make the decision or just a plain old lack of understanding. The latter could be life playing out as it should in order for me to learn and grow.

In this age of self-exploration and self-realization, do you ever delve into why you do the things you do? I regret to admit that in my twenties and thirties, I did not reflect on why I did what I did. I acted and justified any action by telling myself any story that suited my needs. At times, I used my trauma as a justifiable reason as to why I would have outbursts like a babbling brook swelling into an angry river after a torrential downpour.

But I am curious. Have you figured out, Eli, why you didn't make a good impression at times? If you have, did you discover the root cause to make a positive shift towards change? If you have not reflected on this before, I suggest that you do so now because learning why we do what we do is truly eye opening. It is a window into one's heart and soul.

Allow me to share how I explored one of my worst habits. I am embarrassed to admit that I was a yeller, a screamer, a loud person who talked over others. Maybe I used my voice to make me taller than my short 4' 11" stature. I acknowledge it's a weak answer, but I will stand by it for the purpose of sharing this story.

✳✳✳

Early last year, my husband took on a project out west. It was the first time in our 16 years together where we would find ourselves apart from each other for quite some time – six weeks to be exact. We both decided that this was a relatively short period of time in the grand scheme of things; given that the extra money would help fast track our agenda to finish the construction projects around the house. Even when an embraced idea seems straight forward, the result and the imagined outcome typically never match just like the timetable of the train schedule and the time you actually arrive.

The first several days alone were fabulous! I went out to dinner with girlfriends, saw a movie I'd been wanting to see and read a book from the library in peace, without my husband asking me to help him stack wood outside or assist in some other construction chore around the house.

Our initial several days apart were peppered with check-in phone calls that went like this.

"Hi, Hon. What are you doing?"

"How's the weather?"

"Did you get enough sleep?"

Followed by...

"I miss you!"

"I love you!"

After his first full week on the project, he shared elements of the project that were frustrating for him since he likes workflow with process and procedures where the deliverables make the client happy. He does not like finishing work like some off the cuff hack job. I listened and, as this good wife who stepped into the role of fixer, then offered unsolicited suggestions on how to reduce his stress.

Over the next several weeks, he continued to share facets of the project that were more than mere frustrations. He shared the ways his employer changed the scope of work and continued to work on the fly.

When my husband shared that he was not being respected by the employer and belittled in front of his crew, it sent me over the edge emotionally. The crew respected him because he knew how to treat people, handle clients and he had decades of experience not only in telecom and construction but also in sales. I used to joke with my husband that he was the modern-day father of telecommunications, as we know it today in Canada.

Our regular check-in phone calls were no longer filled with curiosity of the job nor pleasantries. Instead they turned into me getting frustrated listening to him relay stories of what was happening at the project.

I want to share that when I get frustrated, I get angry. When I get angry, my body fills with anxiety. Anxiety then turns into unfounded fear and the actions that follow result in me not putting my best foot forward. It's more like foot-in-mouth blunders. What would have been more productive with my foot is to kickbox a sandbag until I figured out what was behind the fear.

On our calls, my anxiety would boil up from my feet, then moved up my body like hot, molten lava. When my anxiety burned past my heart chakra, the pressure would be too much in my internal inferno. I'd explode by yelling at my husband on the phone.

"Why would you allow yourself to be treated that way?"

"Why would you allow them to do this to you?"

"Why this? Why that?"

For four weeks, I did not put my best foot forward during our phone calls and I was ashamed of my behaviour. In times of frustration, there is no time for reflection. I needed someone to hit my reset button because I couldn't do it myself. When our calls finished, the mobile phone would be thrown into the sofa out of anger and this caused unexplained pain for him and for me. I couldn't understand why I couldn't be a supportive wife and just listen to him. My unsolicited suggestions were attempts to fix his situation from afar but were falling on deaf ears and I was frustrated.

Didn't he understand that I was yelling at him to encourage him to make a change either in him or his situation? Didn't he understand I was screaming at him because I loved him? Is that not the craziest thinking, Eli? I scream at my husband because I love him. As I type this to you, I realize how unhealthy and unproductive this habit is and, most of all, it is not an expression of tenderness for someone I love, admire and respect.

Then one night after our most recent call, I wrote in my journal asking myself – what is this all about? Why am I yelling at my husband who loves me? Why am I screaming at a man who is moving our agenda, so we can finish the construction projects at home? He's the one sleeping in a foreign bed while I sleep in our bed. He's the one taking the berating treatment by an employer to financially leap us forward while it would take me 24 months to earn what he would make in 6 weeks. He's the one eating fast food and not working out while I go to my gym regularly and eat home-cooked food made of fresh produce from local farmers. Who was I to treat him this way? He was the one making the sacrifices while I was at home safe and comfortable. He is the one who provides a safe and comfortable home for me. The only people who ever did that for me were my foster parents whom I came to call Mom and Dad.

Once again, as I wrote in my journal, I could feel the anxiety bubble from my feet, up my legs like an angry volcano, rising up through my stomach and when it hit my heart chakra, I started to well up with tears. The tears were the permission I needed to feel again. I placed my pen down on my journal, stood up from my stool at the kitchen island, grasped the island's edge with both hands and let out the loudest, mental, "Wow!" That silenced my body into calm. The tears stopped. I went to the washroom to rinse the salt off my face with cold water, grabbed the towel from the hook beside the sink and buried my face into the towel in shame. I returned the towel to the hook then headed into the living room to retrieve my phone from the sofa where I had thrown it earlier. I took a deep breath, hit the speed dial button to call my husband and waited for him to answer.

When he answered, his greeting was filled with exhaustion and I sensed a plea to not get into another yelling match. I remembered my voice coach saying that sometimes to make a point, it's good to use my inside voice. My inside voice was quieter and nurturing. Heeding that advice, I said, "Honey, I'm sorry that I've been yelling at you for the last four weeks." There was a pause on my end because my ego was sitting on my left shoulder waving its little finger saying don't admit to your failure of being a loving wife. On the right shoulder was an imaginary butterfly opening and closing its wings revealing the choice of transformation.

The silence was then interrupted by my own voice. "I figured out why I've been screaming at you and it's important that you hear what I have to say without interrupting me."

Fear was making my stomach queasy as I continue on, "Please know that I love you and I respect that you're working at a project that may not be the most ideal situation in order to move our agenda forward. After our last call, I wrote in my journal trying to understand why I have been acting that way and now I've figured it out. I was yelling at you because I wanted to be heard. I often feel like I am not heard and when you shared what was going on at work, my body filled with anxiety that eventually turned to fear. I screamed at you because it was the exact same anxiety I felt when I couldn't scream at nine years old when my father molested me. Instead of making myself heard, I laid on my bed confused in silence.

I yelled at you because when I was 12, I told my priest what my father had been doing to me and the priest's response was, "Say an Our Father". I broke my silence by telling someone who I had thought would help me only to be told to say another prayer. I never understood how a prayer was going to make my father stop doing what he did.

I screamed at you because at 14, I told my school counselor what was going on at home and she said, "I'm sorry to hear that. Let's see how the summer goes and we'll deal with it when you return in September." I disclosed to my school counselor, because I expected her to counsel me on how to get out of the situation I was in. Instead, I experienced that summer confused in silence."

My eyes began to well up with tears as I bowed my head in shame and dropped my voice to say in a flat tone of realization, "I screamed at you because I wasn't heard as a child."

Though there were no words coming through the phone for my ear to hear, I knew he was listening to what I was saying because I could hear him taking deep breaths. My words that followed his sigh were, "I'm sorry for my behavior over the last four weeks. It was never you I was upset with. In misplaced anger, I was vocalizing loudly for me, the little girl in me, because the anxiety I felt while listening to you was the same anxiety I felt when I was younger."

I took solace in saying what I had to say over the phone and not face to face because the shame I felt did not contribute to the perceived beauty my husband so often compliments me on. No, shame is ugly. It feels sinful; it looks sinful. Shame is that small scar above the left eye of the past.

My eyes were cast down and he was not even present to bear witness that I could not hold my head up. My head was weighted as the past seemed to be predicting my future. I imagined scenarios where my husband would leave me because he couldn't continue to be married to a woman with these uncontrolled outbursts because of her past. I worried that my husband would choose to stay out west and not come home for the time scheduled or worst case, shaming me into silence once again because of feeling helpless and hopeless. As I lifted my head from the weight of shame, I looked at the living room where we hung drywall together, I saw the hearth in front of the fireplace where we laid tile together, I remembered the countless hours we spent laying, sanding and staining the wood pine floor and a miracle happened…I suddenly felt safe.

The words I finally said with much hope were, "I hope you can forgive me before you come home next week."

I just realized I did the most unthinkable for my hurting heart. I asked for forgiveness from a man that I had yelled at for weeks by not listening to him, empathizing with his situation and not supporting him. Forgiveness was not just for my husband, I gave myself permission to forgive myself for all those years of being stuck confused in silence. This feeling was new for me because it was as if I was touched by the butterfly's grace in that moment.

The silence between us was broken by him asking in his light, jovial voice, "Are you finished?" I nodded my head, then realized he couldn't see me and I said, "Yes." He thanked me, told me he loved me and consoled me as best as he could over the phone. When he was satisfied, that I had calmed down, we said good night and I hit the red button on my phone to end our call.

I placed the phone down on the kitchen island, walked to the bedroom, grabbed Pengy, my stuffed penguin, off the bookshelf, tucked myself into bed without brushing my teeth and fell asleep alone in silence, but no longer confused.

My husband came home for a couple of days after those six weeks but had to go back out west to deal with extended timelines and delayed product deliveries. When we did our check-in calls, I no longer offered unsolicited advice, nor did I continue the negative behavior I had exhibited earlier. I practiced putting my best foot forward by listening and then responding with "I hear that you're frustrated. Well, the project will be over soon."

✳✳✳

Eli, I invite you to reflect when you do not leave a good impression with a loved one or a friend, as those are the hard experiences to delve into. Why? Because you have to feel and be able to walk hand in hand with fear. It is so important to search, explore and discover why you do the things you do, albeit sometimes very difficult.

If you give yourself this permission, have the courage to have empathy for yourself, Eli, and make a shift in how you discover what's inside of you and listen to the words you say to yourself. I did. It's the only way I can practise putting my best foot forward with grace.

In gratitude for listening,

Delane

Hope is a good thing, maybe even the best of things, and good things never die.
– Andy Dufresne (Shawshank Redemption)

CHAPTER 10: NOT MY ANGEL

Dear Eli,

Today is Friday and it's the end of the business day. I'm happy to be on the train heading home. To ensure I don't lose my train of thought, I've pulled out some stationary to share this with you. The week has been somber with the passing of an iconic designer who brought colour to the world and an enthusiast of life who travelled the world and opened his viewer's eyes to a people from many cultures around the world. Both of them took their own lives only days apart from each other. The angst in the air as of late is a result of their passing and once again the raising of mental health awareness.

As I've mentioned in previous letters, triggers can call up dreadfully dismal memories instantly like being on a G4 Network with full bar cell access when searching for something online versus using the old dial-up modem. The memory is front and centre in my mind. Once my row neighbour sat down and arranged his world to his liking, we exchanged glances that suggested you stay in your world and I'll stay in mine, so no one gets hurt. I don't know how passengers have this understood conversation without using words and only the eyes can speak. But it happens. I turned to face the aisle and could feel my Ego sitting on my left shoulder again. As I tried to massage my shoulder to release the knot and make that pesky little gremlin disappear, the dismal memory entered the imaginary stage of my mind.

The song 'Locomotive Breath' comes to mind as our collective seats dance to the rhythm of the wheels rolling along the steel rails. The bouncing of our seats is what keeps me in the present moment as the lyrics play in my head and give me pause to reflect because of my own experience.

Just as it is the space in between the notes where music conjures feelings of love, joy, heartbreak or loss, it's the space in between thoughts and action where magic can happen.

At one point in my twenties, I couldn't get my life right, despite my best efforts. No amount of natural talent I possessed or learned skill I acquired could out-perform the self-hatred I had for myself. Even if there was a 14th Century painter alive today to paint the self-hatred I had for myself, there wouldn't be enough paint nor canvas large enough to hold such a dark visual. Eli, what I'm about to share with you has only been shared with select friends in conversation when I felt safe. Putting this on paper makes this very uncomfortable for me. But I will share for maybe you'll appreciate my perception of respect for life.

✸✸✸

On one summer day after work, I was walking down a street with no particular place to go. There was no cool breeze to keep me present. What I recall is the sun's brightness reflecting off the white, cement sidewalk making it difficult for my eyes to absorb my surroundings. Since I could not afford sunglasses, I squinted my eyes to limit the light intake that was giving me a slight headache. Headaches and migraines were normal in my body, so this day's physical sensation was just an annoyance.

As I crossed the street and the sound of cars got louder, the memories of Tatay came rushing back like a ghost whispering each memory of touch back into my body. With each whisper, the shame in my soul escorted in each horrific memory which consumed my entire being. The avalanche of heinous acts by Tatay was burying me mentally and I felt it necessary to escape my physical body. At this moment in time, it felt paramount because I saw no other way to cleanse my body or mind, so that I could believe I was worthy to live. There was too much memory taking over. It was like being lost in Mussorgsky's Pictures at an Exhibition Movement No. 8 'The Catacombs'.

I had made previous attempts at ridding my body of physical memories but they were thwarted by not taking enough codeine pills in relation to my body weight, coupled with not being bright enough to include other chemicals to complete the task. That was then and this is now. As I continued to walk, my pace picked up in the hopes that the memories would somehow not catch up with my physical being. What a fool I was for thinking that I could rid my body of memory. A bead of sweat came down my hairline and hung on my chin line for a brief moment then dropped on to the sidewalk. I hit my forehead with the palm of my left hand for being so stupid in thinking that I was anything that's right or anyone who could be loved. Love was a lie. Love does not heal the world. Love does not care for little children.

I took one step closer to the guardrail, and, without a thought, placed my right hand on the rail, as I was about to do my layup over and onto the highway below. Out of nowhere, a hand was placed over my right shoulder and I heard someone whisper in my left ear, "You might be ready to die today, but the people below are not." I gasped ever so slowly, removing my hand from the rail. When I turned around, no one was there, only the cars passing by on the overpass we shared. Like a shamed hyena who's intended kill escaped, I hurried off the overpass and continued on to find a park bench.

I curled myself up into a ball on the corner of the bench rocking myself back and forth as I did when I was a child to tell myself I'd be ok. The realization that set in on top of my own shame is that I did not consider the other people. I almost killed others at the expense of my own selfish intention. I sat there for hours until the cool chill of the evening brought calm over my body and enabled me to return home.

That night, I phoned a friend to tell her I made another suicide attempt and she interrupted me by saying, "Go ahead and kill yourself. I'm sick of these calls. Just know this…if you go through with it, I will not come to your funeral." Distraught I hung up on her. Hearing those words from a friend I counted on and knew since childhood made me lose hope; hope that I was salvageable. I was good at giving up on people for people gave up on me. For some reason though, I never stopped searching for that someone who would have hope for me; hope that I would pull through past my trauma and 'make it' whatever that meant.

✹✹✹

Eli, so many years have passed since that experience but what I interpreted from that phone call was that I was no longer worthy of a friend. What is interesting is that my body recorded the strong staccato of her words, the vibration of her voice and I carried it with me through many rough experiences. It manifested itself in the deeply-held belief that I was unworthy of care. Then, I realized that escaping this mammalian vessel despite the mental noise did not matter because, whether I was dead or alive, no one cared so I may as well face whatever came my way.

I find it interesting that, as I re-read the last sentence, I'm sure there were people who cared for me but unfortunately, they were out-numbered by my made-up ghosts and the imagined people who I thought I would encounter. Yes, imaginary beings outweighed the real number of people who did care such as my foster mother who took me in. I needed to find a way to truly believe that I was worthy of care meaning self-care.

Whether we acknowledge it or not, time does offer us the opportunity to grow, heal and change. The passing of time allowed me to learn that people did care, but more importantly, I needed to care about myself. I realized that it was only then that my life would change. It's really too bad there was no book or manual given to me for my sixteenth birthday warning me how trauma would wreak havoc in my life.

In addition, Eli, I want to share my experience with the voice I had heard on the overpass. Do you remember when I said earlier that it's the space in between thoughts and actions where magic can happen? For years I have told myself that it was an angel who whispered those words into my ear to prevent me from jumping.

I have even romanticized that it was my guardian angel. However, I have also wondered if it was someone else's guardian angel who was letting me know that I could have taken someone else's life along with mine: maybe a mother, father, doctor, friend or child. From this experience, I've learned to have a healthy respect for life and time. The time that we all have is finite so who am I to deny myself or anyone else their life or their contribution to society.

Do I fear death? I'm not sure. I can say that I fear that I may not have enough time to accomplish all that I am meant to do. So, I have challenged myself to be the best me I can be and to be conscious and conscientious in all of my choices.

Eli, I still have some time before arriving at the train station so I'm going to take a nap. This letter may have been short, but I'll say this…it's no light matter to share the story of wanting to take one's own life. I am grateful that my life was saved on that day.

In gratitude for listening,

Delane

Loving yourself does not mean being self-absorbed or narcissistic, or disregarding others. Rather it means welcoming yourself as the most honored guest in your own heart, a guest worthy of respect, a lovable companion.
– Margo Anand

CHAPTER 11: POLLUTION

Dear Eli,

Today is Thursday and I'm on my way home. Now that I have my tea, I am settled in my little train world with my stationary out to write you another letter. Hopefully, my handwriting is legible. For some reason, for the last several weeks on Thursdays, the passengers, myself included, have had the unwelcome treat of riding this older train car that requires new shock absorbers. Last week, the service attendant almost lost control of her cart that would have emptied its top contents onto the person across the way from me. Fortunately, myself and another passenger helped her steady the cart. I must say the train ride feels like a kiddie roller coaster ride sometimes, but I digress.

On my way to the station, I passed a guy running on Front Street and noted that I envied him for his afternoon run. Personally, I'm not a runner and never have been. Do you run, Eli? Truth be told, I was never into sports at all. I did them as a child because my friends participated in sports and I wanted to belong and be part of the team. For most my life, I haven't worked out or done anything physical outside of walking. Then, my husband and I met a friend who introduced us to Downward Dog Yoga. Since then we've been practicing yoga not for the sheer physical strength but for the holistic well being of the mind and body. Recently, I decided to take up boxing. Why? Well, I'm working on a large art project that will require me to be mentally and physically strong. The club I belong to started to offer boxing and I decided to sign up. Having never met the boxing instructor, I asked the gym director for his email so I could share with him my reason for signing up. I learned in yoga that when I take a class with a new instructor it's important to inform him/her any injuries or soreness I may have. I sent him an email about the art project I was working on and received a very positive reply with one word, "EXCELLENT". I am going to share snippets of my boxing experience with you, Eli, because something profound happened to me during the first eight weeks with my boxing coach.

❋❋❋

To prepare for my session, I went to a place on Yonge Street that sold boxing gloves. When I entered the store, the clerk behind the counter smiled and thought I was lost and coming in to ask for directions. As I approached the counter, I could see sets of boxing gloves in the glass case, but they all seemed humungous as though they were made for a Sasquatch! The man didn't bother to get up from his bar stool as he asked if he could help me. When I asked for gloves, he chuckled and suggested I get the size he offered because it would have more padding for my hands. Not knowing any better, I shrugged my shoulders and agreed since what he said seemed to make sense. He advised me that I needed wraps too, so I paid for both items and felt happy with my purchase. When I got to the car, my husband asked to see my purchase and he laughed saying, 'Don't you think those are too big for you, honey?' I told him what the man behind the counter said. He shrugged his shoulders, too, as if in agreement.

Three days later, I entered the gym for my first one-on-one boxing session. Several minutes later, the boxing instructor walked in and introduced himself as Isac. Our first session together was an assessment of my cardio stamina, physical strength and knowledge of boxing. I don't recall which session it was. Perhaps it was my third or fourth session when Isac asked how my art project was going while we were in the middle of warming up. I shook my head indicating that it wasn't going well and that I didn't want to talk. I just wanted to physically release the tension inside me. After a brief run, several rounds of jumping jacks and rope skipping, it was time to put my gloves on. Sensing I was not in a good headspace, he coached me through the punches on the punching bag. 'Jab, jab, left uppercut, right uppercut. Do it again. Jab, jab, left uppercut, right uppercut. Again. Again.

Again.' Whatever combination of punches he instructed, I followed. My focus was hitting that bag and thinking of nothing else. Every time he said, "Again" I obeyed.

Then, in the midst of one of the combination of punches I realized that I was no longer seeing the bag. I was seeing Tatay. I could hear Isac's voice in the distance, but what was in front of me was the opportunity to deliver powerful physical blows to the imagined body in front of me. I was taking every uppercut and jab I could. I was releasing years of hurt, anger and frustration. Then, when the right hook contacted the bag, I bent over with gloves on my knees and I started crying so deeply that my chest was heaving.

Isac asked, "What's up? Speak to me." The gym was full of other people so I tried my best to be quiet but my tears flowed and I cried, "I hate that this happened to me. I hate that I have to be brave. I hate that I live with the memories." "That's why you're here, Delane. To get through it. Not to hate. To get through it. You can't change the past, right?" He told me to stand straight up then looked me in the eye and continued, "Right?" 'Yes, you're right," I said as I worked to pull myself together, I grabbed the towel on the floor with my gloves still on and did my best to wipe my face of the tears and sweat.

I had thought, with all the work I'd been doing working through my pain that I was able to handle my trauma. With boxing, it was apparent that trauma wasn't finished with me despite me being finished with it. The more I moved during boxing, the more trauma trash surfaced. The thing with trauma trash is that it rises and collects at the surface. It contaminates the mind just as pollution poisons the ocean. Both cannot be ignored. They must be dealt with. Hitting a punching bag helped release the sea of emotion.

We finished up the session with a sparring match as Isac brought me back to present by taunting me with, "C'mon you can do better than that. Is that all you got?" The punches I had laid on the imaginary Tatay along with the emotional release drained most of my physical energy, so our sparring session became quite hilarious. Isac would taunt me and I would laugh. It takes a good coach to allow a pupil to go through the exercises, but it takes a great coach to allow the pupil to experience emotion, give it permission to come out and use that emotion for positive motivation. When our session finished Isac asked, "You're working on your art project today, right?" I smiled and gave him two thumbs up.

※※※

After that session, Eli, I went to St. James Park nearby to reflect on what happened in the gym. As I sat on the park bench staring at the water fountain and the birds bathing, it dawned on me that I was still incredibly angry with Tatay and I had never expressed that anger physically. I've only expressed my anger on paper or at other people when triggered. The latter realization was an uncomfortable truth. It was at that moment that I accepted and gave myself permission to be angry.

※※※

I noticed that, with each training session with Isac, I was given the opportunity to be different versions of myself as I was growing up to express my anger. I could be that child who was taken advantage of or the adult version of myself who was told I wasn't a woman. Isac taught me that what comes out in the gym stays in the gym. There is no need to carry it with me neither to the locker room nor out into the world. Today's session was no different than the previous boxing trainings except that today my attitude changed. The running, rope skipping and weights from the previous session were making me physically and mentally strong.

I started to believe that I could handle anything that came my way. That is…until yesterday. Yesterday I had a call from a woman through an introduction of a friend. Our mutual friend thought that it would be good for us to connect since we both, in our own ways, were trying to make a difference in the world in helping improve the lives of children. It's interesting, Eli, how people who have similar childhood experiences of trauma can get right down to the nitty-gritty very matter of fact part of a shared experience. We can ask about and state what happened without emotion or tears being shed. As we both spoke about our pasts, the statistics of childhood sexual abuse and the people we know who experienced similar trauma, it really hit me that my story was the story of many; too many.

After our phone call, which didn't last more than 45 minutes, I closed my eyes because I was completely fatigued from hearing the numbers. Behind the curtain of my eyes, the canister of film for my life came out. It was strewn on the imaginary floor of my mind along with the visual of thousands upon thousands of film reels all telling a collective story of pain and sadness. What was interesting though was that some of the rolls of film had halos of light around them. They were not the stories of lost souls who could never find the light through all of the trauma and pain. They were not the stories of those who, themselves, became abusers. Instead they were stories of hope. Right then and there I knew that was the story I wanted to tell.

When I got into the gym, I put my wraps on. Isac had not yet arrived. I stood in the gym alone and looked at the mirror to see the reflection of me and no one else. It was the first time I actually saw my whole body in a mirror alone.

✲✲✲

As strange as this may sound, Eli, it was as if I wasn't looking at me. I was looking at a stranger, someone who was strong and courageous. Could I accept myself as someone who is that strong? Am I courageous? Just who was that person I was looking at in the mirror?

✲✲✲

The door opened to the gym and Isac walked into room. He noticed I was contemplating something, so he asked with a good morning smile, "What's going on in that head of yours?"

As we warmed up in front of the mirror, I told him about the phone call I had and what I was thinking about before he walked in. It was natural for me to share these thoughts with Isac because he was able to take my thoughts and break them down in bite-sized chunks for me to decipher what was really going on in my mind. That, Eli, is a true gift! When I told him that I questioned if I was courageous, there was no hesitation in his reply, "Of course, you are!" With that he had me on the bag practicing combos and then we sparred. He was getting me to push my body like I had never consciously pushed it before. When we finished I picked up my towel, keys and water to go and he said, "Hey, don't forget....it takes courage to show up every day. You do." I smiled and turned to go to the locker room.

While in the steam room, I reflected on the last several weeks of boxing with Isac. It occurred to me the gym was a great training ground to learn about self-acceptance and it continues to be a healthy place to do so. What was surprising to me was the sheer number of physical memories that had been pent up inside.

✳✳✳

Physical exercise was the catalyst to put those memories under pressure like molten lava in order to explode out of this volcano. I am grateful for the many people who have come into my life but the one that stands out is my teacher of life disguised as a boxing coach named Isac.

One of these days, Eli, I hope you'll share with me a teacher who has been a catalyst in your life. It would be lovely to learn about you in this way if you are open to sharing.

It's time for me to pack up since we are nearing the station.

In gratitude,

Delane

Real transformation requires real honesty. If you want to move forward – get real with yourself.
– Bryant McGill

CHAPTER 12: A KNIGHT'S HUG

Dear Eli,

Today is Monday and believe it or not the train arrived on time. This morning, the reddish orange ball of fire rising above the trees was a sight to behold. It's the kind of sunrise that makes me realize how lucky I am to witness something so beautiful. Speaking of luck, I'd like to share with you an experience that happened over the weekend. No, I didn't win the lottery; so let's take that off the table.

On Saturday, my husband and I watched a movie called, "Flight of the Butterflies." It's a story of discovery – the story of the monarch butterfly, its migration, and the dedication of Dr. Fred Urquhart and his wife, Norah. If you ever get a chance to watch the film, I do recommend it, because one of messages is that in order to find truth, it takes time, patience and dedication, which leads me to my story of luck and truth.

✳✳✳

On Sunday morning, my husband and I did our morning routine of coffee, reading the news and then me in the kitchen with the fridge open pondering what to make for breakfast. With the door open in my left hand, I felt an arm come from behind me on my left side and an arm over my right shoulder and bam – there was a hug. I jumped, turned around and stammered, "Don't do that!"

What started off as a beautiful morning, took a 180-degree turn after I reprimanded my husband for expressing his love. I had jumped back and scolded him in a sharp tone. When our eyes met, after my outburst, I could see the hurt in his eyes and he replied with a bit of sadness in his voice, "I was only giving you a hug. It's not like I'm some stranger." With that he turned around, grabbed his phone off the kitchen counter and sat on the sofa hoping the phone's screen would provide some magical answer as to why he couldn't hug his own wife.

In all our years of marriage, I never questioned why I would jump with fear every time he tried to hug me. I made breakfast, served it and we sat in silence eating. It's truly an uncomfortable environment when two people sit at the same table, acknowledge each other's presence but no words are spoken. Since I am not well practiced at apologizing to my husband, I maintained our little charade of civility in silence. It was childish on my part and that's when I caught the full mental conversation I was having with myself. The word 'childish' caught my attention.

After our meals were finished, he went into the bedroom and closed the door. When he emerged he didn't even look my way as I was still at the kitchen island. He was dressed to be on the tractor as he continued on through the hallway to the foyer. I heard the closet door open, shut and then the front door open and close. There was no slamming of the front door, no anger expressed. There was just the quiet sound of the mechanism of the door catching the clasp. I surmised he was going to take down several red cedars on the north end of the lot.

Taking a deep breath, I wished Pearlaso were still alive. She was our beautiful Portuguese Waterdog who was a constant companion. It's been two years since Pearlaso passed away and she was usually the catalyst that could bring us back together again without any explanations of why we behaved the way we did.

For over a decade, I never addressed sensitive issues because Pearlaso was an incredible distraction that could melt away any hurt or pain whether from my past or a spat with my husband. Did every single one need to be addressed, sliced, diced, analyzed and resolved? The story I told myself was not really, not every spat needed to be resolved. But this particular one was different because I have let this one go on far too long. Scolding my husband for expressing his love was completely out of line and the word 'childish' was the hook that got me thinking.

As I washed the dishes and cleaned up the rest of the kitchen I went into my bedroom and picked up my journal and the first word I wrote was childish. Then I rewrote the word over and over again filling a page. Page two of the journal was filled with child-ish. On page three, I asked myself what the connection between what happened today and what happened when I was a child was? Then I looked up the suffix 'ish' meaning 'belonging to', 'after the manner of' and 'having characteristics of'.

✹✹✹

'Belonging to' resonated throughout my body and Eli, I fervently wrote in my journal for another hour.

✹✹✹

Have you ever tried to break something down to understand it and really get to the root of it? I had mentioned previously that we have to have the courage to search, explore and discover why we do the things we do. I owed it to myself to figure out why I was behaving that way. I also owed it to my husband. Why was I not allowing him to express his love through a simple hug?

Triggers happen regularly for me, but sometimes I don't recognize them as triggers. I sometimes chalk them up to likes or dislikes and it's just the way it is because I said so. It's also easy for someone like me to think an action is absolute such as his hug. When I reflected over the years of our marriage, there were many moments where we hugged, but now I had to figure out why some hugs were ok and others not. I had to figure out the truth, just like in the butterfly documentary. As a result of watching the movie, I decided to write down the hugs I could remember that were happy and tried to recall the more recent times when they were not so positive, similar to our exchange this morning. Next to the happy hugs with my husband, I wrote down all the feelings that I associated with the positive hugs, which were safety, love, joy, laughter and peace. Then I allowed myself the gift of feeling the fear. The fear came from remembering the feelings that went with each negative hug.

✹✹✹

This exercise, Eli, was not easy because I dislike remembering the feelings that make me feel scared but I was able to talk myself through it.

***

No one was around to witness whatever was going to come out so I reviewed the negative hug list once again and closed my eyes. I reminded myself to let things happen 'pole, pole; slowly, slowly.'

Feelings of pain, hurt, abandonment, abuse, darkness and shame came into my body and behind the lids of my eyes I could see the truth about the fear. It was the truth of having been picked up and thrown down onto the bed. The times of unwanted touch came streaming through my mind and body. Those painful memories flooded my senses and I began to well up with tears. I had to bear witness to every moment of unwanted touch that my memory could recall; from Tatay to each boyfriend to strangers on the street. When the film reel of memories stopped, I opened my eyes, took a deep breath in and let out a big sigh of relief. I survived feeling the feelings. Instantly, a sense of peace came over me like the experience of being at the top of Mt. Kilimanjaro. By experiencing peace, I could see the truth – I was holding our marriage back because I was allowing my past to affect my present. Eli, that was an "aha" moment for me! After soaking in this sense of acceptance, I went into the washroom to rinse the salt off my face from all the salty soldiers that I had shed.

Later that afternoon, I invited my husband to join me in the living room to see if he would be open to listening to what I had to say. I wanted to apologize and explain myself about what happened earlier in the morning. When we sat, I could feel the heat of shame go up my spine, but I faced him with the best smile I could muster, despite my eyes welling up with tears. I spoke my apology in this way,

"I'm sorry I yelled at you this morning when you tried to hug me. I know you are trying to show me how much you love me through a hug. I have only now figured out why I freak out when you hug me. The times you hug me and we're face to face I don't recall anything bad because I can see you and I know you love me. It's the times when you hug me from behind and I can't see you that trigger me. I know you think it's ok but it's not because I perceive it as unwanted touch despite knowing that you would never hurt me. I can't seem to separate the fact that it's you and the memories my body recalls.

So, in a slow, calm voice he asked, "So what do we do?"

I started to feel uncomfortable because I had identified the root of the problem but I had not thought of a solution to offer. I sat quietly for what seemed like a long time and then I came up with "I would like you to ask permission, especially if I can't see you and I don't know what's coming." I took a deep breath in and let it out as I waited for his response.

With a smile filled with hope he said, "Ok. So, can I have a hug now?" I nodded my head indicating yes and I hugged him tight. I hugged him because I knew how much he loved me. I allowed myself to be in his arms because I felt safe. I allowed us to be in each other's arms because we loved each other and I knew things were going to be ok.

✻✻✻

So, Eli, you might wonder what luck had to do with the weekend? I was lucky to watch a movie about a caterpillar going through a metamorphosis to become a monarch butterfly and a man's journey that sought out the truth of the monarch's migration. Also, as luck would have it, my husband was patient enough with me so I could seek the truth through my own metamorphosis and I am grateful that he did. His action, Eli, is what I've come to learn is love expressed through a hug.

I look forward to the day when we connect to reminisce, laugh and share stories together.

In gratitude,

Delane

THE TWINE

~~Dear Eli,~~

~~Today is Thursday and it's been quite some time since I've written.~~

Dear Journal,

Today is Thursday. Last night I my husband approached me with a stack of letters that were tied together by twine. I had meant to stuff them into my backpack and take the stack of letters to the studio but, silly me, I was in a hurry and left them on the sofa. He didn't go through the letters but noticed each envelope had the name Eli; no last name and no address just the name Eli.

As you can imagine, he asked if there was another man and I said, 'Let me pour us a glass of wine and explain who Eli really is.'

When we sat down I explained that Eli was short for Elizabeth. Having had a hysterectomy, I always thought I would like to have adopted a daughter and name her Elizabeth. I would call her Eli pronounced 'ee-lye'. Around the time when I was 18, a friend named Jon was dating a woman whose nickname was Eli. When he showed me a photo of her, I knew that, if I ever had a daughter, she'd be named after this woman. The petite woman in the photo had short black hair, green eyes and skin like porcelain. She was wearing a black leather fitted jacket and faded blue jeans with the Pacific Ocean crashing behind her. What I saw in the photo was a woman of incredible presence who exuded strength, courage and beauty. When I asked my friend Jon why she went by Eli he explained that she grew up with four brothers and her father wanted her to be as strong as her siblings. He nicknamed her Eli so her brothers would treat her the same and not pick on her.

Seeing that my husband was trying to be patient with my story I opened a letter for him to see for himself and said, 'Look, I made Eli up. She's not real. I don't have a secret daughter out there and I don't have some secret lover out there. I wrote these letters pretending that if I had a daughter these are the things I would I say to her. Mothers and fathers write letters to their newborn babies so I thought I'd do the same as an exercise to heal."

I randomly selected another letter, opened the letter of my climb to Mt. Kilimanjaro and read it out loud. His body language changed from disbelief to love. When asked what he thought, he replied with tenderness, "It's hard to listen to and know these things happened to you."

With the letter still in hand, I continued, "These are the stories I wanted to share if I did have a daughter - stories of growth, self-acceptance and transformation. I considered burning the letters but later thought maybe I'd pass them on to my nieces so they could learn more about me. Or truth be told I'd keep them around and read them once in a while to remind myself of who I am. These letters were written to the child in me; the child who never got to be a child; the child I took care of and carried with me into adulthood. I wrote these letters so I could accept me in the hopes that I would learn to love myself. And you know what? I do love me because of what I've discovered from writing these letters. You, Mom and Dad have taught me that I do deserve love and in return I learn on a regular basis how to love. And you know what is a surprising discovery? I really do matter.'

> *"You can't go back and change the beginning*
> *but you can start where you are and*
> *change the ending."*
> – C.S. Lewis

AFTERWORD

This book was written to help the reader open their mind to the experiences of people who endured childhood sexual abuse. It is the story of the pain and emotion that some people experience as they walk through their lives. It is not just my story, but the story of many.

Writing this book has allowed me to have more empathy for myself and other people who have experienced trauma. I have lived many years with shame and guilt because of the stories I told myself about me and the people around me.

These letters to my inner child, Eli, were the conversations I wish I could have had with myself along the way. However, time has allowed me to heal and I am glad I have the stories now. This writing has been a journey of self-discovery and learning what it means to practice healthy boundaries, self-care and to celebrate me being me. It is my hope that you were open to learning about my growth and that you can grow from some of my experiences. Maybe there has been the opportunity for you, the reader, to self-reflect and learn about yourself too. I have shared these letters so we may learn about each other and ourselves in this life so we may have the courage to heal and embrace life beyond the pain.

Made in the USA
Middletown, DE
25 March 2019